CRIMINAL INJURIES COMPENSATION CLAIMS 2008

Related titles from Law Society Publishing:

Civil Litigation Handbook (2nd edn)
General Editor: District Judge Suzanne Burn, Consultant Editor: Professor John Peysner

Conditional Fees (3rd edn)
Gordon Wignall, Consultant Editor: Steven Green

Criminal Injuries Compensation Claims
Clare Padley and Laura Begley

Domestic Abuse
Jane Wilson

Personal Injury Handbook
Nicholas Waller

Titles from Law Society Publishing can be ordered from all good bookshops or direct (telephone 0870 850 1422, email lawsociety@prolog.uk.com or visit our online shop at www.lawsociety.org.uk/bookshop).

CRIMINAL INJURIES COMPENSATION CLAIMS 2008

A Guide to the New Scheme

Laura Begley, Aileen Downey and Clare Padley

The Law Society

ISBN–13: 978–1–85328-829–6

Please refer to **www.cica.gov.uk** for the most up-to-date versions of the material reproduced in the appendices.

Published in 2010 by the Law Society
113 Chancery Lane, London WC2A 1PL

Typeset by Columns Design Ltd, Reading
Printed by Hobbs the Printers Ltd, Totton, Hants

The paper used for the text pages of this book is FSC certified. FSC (the Forest Stewardship Council) is an international network to promote responsible management of the world's forests.

CONTENTS

APPENDICES

FOREWORD

It is five years since the publication of *Criminal Injuries Compensation Claims* by Clare Padley and Laura Begley (Law Society, 2005). This handbook is now established as the textbook of choice for all who are concerned with claims under the statutory Schemes. Practitioners, the Criminal Injuries Compensation Authority (CICA) and Tribunal judges and members all find it an invaluable source of information and guidance.

Claims for compensation received after 3 November 2008 will be considered under the Criminal Injuries Compensation Scheme 2008. There are a number of important differences between the 2008 Scheme and the earlier Schemes. In addition there have been a number of significant changes to the appeals process under the 2008 Scheme. Appeals against a decision of the CICA are now made to the First-tier Tribunal (Criminal Injuries Compensation) which has replaced the Criminal Injuries Appeals Panel. The First-tier Tribunal is an independent panel which was set up by the Tribunals, Courts and Enforcement Act 2007.

Whilst the make up of the Tribunal is similar to the earlier Panel, all appeals, including those under the earlier Schemes, are now subject to the Tribunal Procedure (First-tier Tribunal) (Social Entitlement Chamber) Rules 2008. These Rules introduce a new formality into the appeals process and appellants and practitioners will need to be familiar them and to abide by them.

The 2008 Scheme has some important differences from the earlier Schemes. Apart from a new tariff of injuries, there are also a number of areas where there has been a tightening-up of the wording to the Scheme. For example, circumstances under which time limits may be waived are stricter and there is a significant change to the wording of the 2008 Scheme in relation to care claims under paragraph 35(d)(iii).

This book also deals with the Rules for appeal hearings and highlights the most important changes to the appeals process for all parties to consider.

Criminal Injuries Compensation Claims 2008 is essential reading for all involved in criminal injury compensation claims. Together with the original 2005 handbook, this new volume must be on the bookshelf of everyone who intends to advise a victim of a crime of violence. The decision-makers at the CICA will need to be familiar with its contents, and this book will also be added to the libraries of all Tribunal judges and members, and I expect to see copy at every appeal hearing.

However, I must repeat my predecessor's note of caution – unless there has been an error of law, it is the Tribunal's decision, not the books' content, that is final!

Tony Summers
Principal Judge
First-tier Tribunal – Criminal Injuries Compensation
April 2010

PREFACE

It is now 5 years since *Criminal Injuries Compensation Claims* was published (Law Society, 2005).

The main change since then is the introduction of the 2008 Scheme, and the accompanying procedural rules which apply to all current appeals.

Our aim in writing this supplementary book is to deal with the changes resulting from the new Scheme and the rules, and to provide practical guidance to assist users of the 2008 Scheme in achieving the best results.

We have also endeavoured to include up-to-date case law and legislation where this has materially affected the implementation of the Schemes generally.

This book reflects the Schemes and relevant case law as at April 2010.

We should stress that, save where expressly stated in the text, the views and opinions expressed in this book are not to be taken as having the approval of the CICA or the Tribunal, and any errors or omissions are entirely our own.

We would like to thank our editor Janet Noble and her team for all their support and hard work throughout this process.

We are also extremely grateful to Tony Summers, the current Principal Judge of the Tribunal, for taking the time to read the book and for providing the foreword.

Laura Begley
April 2010

TABLE OF CASES

TABLE OF STATUTES

Statutory instruments

PART 1 **ELIGIBILITY**

1 INTRODUCTION

1.1 USING THIS BOOK

In this book, we aim to provide a general guide to the Criminal Injuries Compensation Scheme 2008 (referred to in this book as 'the 2008 Scheme'). This book should be read in conjunction with *Criminal Injuries Compensation Claims* by Clare Padley and Laura Begley (Law Society, 2005), which contains a more detailed analysis of criminal injuries compensation claims generally. We hope that this book, alongside the 2005 handbook and the Guide to the Criminal Injuries Compensation Scheme 2008' ('the 2008 Scheme Guide', **Appendix 2** to this book), will assist practitioners in understanding the provisions of the new 2008 Scheme. For ease of reference the structure of this book follows the structure of the 2005 handbook.

1.2 OVERVIEW OF THE 2008 SCHEME

The 2008 Scheme governs all applications received by the Criminal Injuries Compensation Authority (CICA) on or after 3 November 2008. The 2008 Scheme makes limited but significant changes to the previous 2001 and 1996 Schemes.

1.2.1 Eligibility

The 2008 Scheme applies the same criteria in respect of eligibility as in the 2001 Scheme, so there is no change in the definition of criminal injury, or personal injury, and the exceptional risk category remains. The £500,000 cap also remains. Full details of these eligibility criteria are set out in *Criminal Injuries Compensation Claims*, Chapters 2–7, and the most recent developments in this field are outlined in **Chapter 2** of this book.

1.2.2 Failure to report or cooperate

The CICA can still reduce or withhold an award if the applicant fails to report to the police, fails to cooperate with the police, other authorities or the CICA, or on account of the applicant's conduct before or after the incident or in relation to the applicant's character as evidenced by any convictions. The 2008 Scheme Guide suggests that a reduction on account of criminal convictions is mandatory now. An additional ground for withholding an award has been included at paragraph 14(1) for situations where 'the applicant has repeatedly and without reasonable excuse' failed to respond to the CICA's communications at his or her last known address.

1.2.3 Assessment of compensation

The 2008 Scheme still retains the tariff scheme for injury awards, but with a new tariff, although some awards are unchanged. See **Chapter 3** for details of these changes. The other key changes relate to the way damages and deductions may be calculated in acceleration claims. Also, there are changes in respect of the basis for care claims and ancillary expenses arising out of the administration of awards for those who lack mental capacity. See **Chapter 5** for details of these changes. Full details of the unchanged provisions for the assessment of compensation are set out in *Criminal Injuries Compensation Claims*, Chapters 8–12.

1.2.4 Time limits

Paragraph 18 tightens up the time limit requirement. A two-year limitation period still applies but a claims officer may now only waive the limit where:

(a) it is practicable for the application to be considered; and
(b) in the particular circumstances of the case, it would not have been reasonable to expect the applicant to have made an application within the two-year period.

See **Chapter 7** for details of this and other minor procedural changes. Full details of the unchanged provisions for the procedure involved in criminal injuries compensation claims are set out in *Criminal Injuries Compensation Claims*, Chapters 13–21.

1.2.5 New appellate body

The CICA still determines the application, but now if the application is refused or the applicant is unhappy with the award, an appeal can be made to the First-tier Tribunal (Criminal Injuries Compensation), (referred to in this book as the 'First-tier Tribunal' or 'Tribunal'), which replaces the previous appellate body, the Criminal Injuries Compensation Appeals Panel (CICAP). This First-tier Tribunal is an independent panel, set up by the Tribunals, Courts and Enforcement Act 2007. The Tribunal will be composed of legally qualified judges, medically qualified members and lay members, and the usual composition of a Tribunal will be one Judge and two members, one of whom is medically qualified. See **Chapters 10** and **11** and **Appendix 3**.

1.2.6 New procedural rules

A key change is in relation to the procedure governing appeals, which is now set out in the Tribunal Procedure (First-tier Tribunal) (Social Entitlement Chamber) Rules 2008, SI 2008/2685 (the 'Tribunal Procedure Rules': see **Chapters 10** and **11** and

Appendix 3). These rules are supplemented by practice guidance issued by the Principal Judge in November 2008, which can be found at **Appendix 4**.

2 CRIMES OF VIOLENCE AND OTHER ELIGIBILITY CRITERIA

2.1 INTRODUCTION

Eligibility is dealt with by paragraphs 6–17 of the 2008 Scheme. As with the 2001 and 1996 Schemes, in order to apply for compensation under the 2008 Scheme, the applicant must be eligible to receive an award. Compensation may be payable to an applicant who has suffered a criminal injury after 1 August 1964, or to a qualifying claimant, where a victim of a criminal injury sustained after that date has since died. The injury must be sustained in and directly attributable to an act occurring in Great Britain (Northern Ireland is covered by a different Scheme), although the jurisdiction is extended to cover criminal injuries sustained on board British aircraft and ships (see Notes 1 and 2 of the 2008 Scheme).

2.2 CRIMINAL INJURIES

As in the 1996 and 2001 Schemes, paragraph 6 of the 2008 Scheme provides that compensation may be paid to an applicant who has sustained a criminal injury on or after 1 August 1964, or to a qualifying claimant where a victim of a criminal injury sustained on or after 1 August 1964 has since died.

2.2.1 Criminal injury

Criminal injury is defined in paragraph 8 of the 2008 Scheme in similar terms to the previous Schemes to mean:

> one or more personal injuries [...] being an injury sustained in and directly attributable to an act occurring in Great Britain [...] which is:
>
> (a) a crime of violence (including arson, fire-raising or an act of poisoning); or
> (b) an offence of trespass on a railway; or
> (c) the apprehension or attempted apprehension of an offender or a suspected offender, the prevention or attempted prevention of an offence, or the giving of help to any constable who is engaged in any such activity.

The authors note that the order of the words in this provision has been slightly changed, so that it is now clear that both the injury and the incident to which the injury is directly attributable must occur within Great Britain. This change may be a consequence of arguments being raised over whether the wording of paragraph 6 of the previous Schemes allowed for a claim to be made where an applicant sustained an injury (such as a mental injury) in Great Britain as a consequence of an incident (such as a murder) which took place abroad. Such a claim would not be allowed under the new wording of paragraph 6. Personal injury is defined further in paragraph 9 of the 2008 Scheme and further restrictions on eligibility are detailed in paragraphs 10–12 of the 2008 Scheme. There has been no change in the definitions of criminal injury or personal injury, or indeed what amounts to exceptional risk under paragraph 12 of the Scheme.

That said, the authors wish to make it clear that the House of Lords decision in *R* v. *G & R* [2003] UKHL 50 has superseded the decision in *R* v. *Caldwell* [1982] AC 341. As a result of this, where *Criminal Injuries Compensation Claims* (Law Society, 2005) suggested at paragraph 2.4.2 that the *mens rea* in the offence of criminal damage or arson was the objective test per *R* v. *Caldwell* [1982] AC 341,this was an error for which the authors apologise. The House of Lords in *R* v. *G & R* held that the Court of Appeal had erred in *R* v. *Caldwell* in concluding that the meaning of recklessness under the Criminal Damage Act 1971 did not include proof of foresight of injury with the accused then going on to take this risk. The facts in *R* v. *G & R* illustrate the point nicely. Two boys aged 11 and 12 went camping without their parents' permission. They set fire to newspapers which they put under a wheelie bin in a yard at the rear of a shop. They assumed that the papers would burn themselves out. However, the wheelie bin caught fire and the fire spread to the shop causing over £1 million worth of damage. Neither boy appreciated the risk of the fire spreading. They were convicted at first instance and on appeal in reliance on the objective test in *R* v. *Caldwell*. The reversal of that decision and imposition of the partially subjective test in *R* v. *Cunningham* [1957] 2 QB 396 resulted in their convictions being quashed by the House of Lords. The test under Criminal Damage Act 1971, s.1 is formulated thus: a person acted recklessly within the meaning of the Act with respect to (i) a circumstance when he was aware of a risk that it existed or would exist; and (ii) a result when he was aware of a risk that it would occur and it was in the circumstances known to him unreasonable to take the risk. In our view, this does not alter the law in respect of the need for hostile intent in determining whether there has been a crime of violence. See paragraphs 2.4 and 2.7 of *Criminal Injuries Compensation Claims* (Law Society, 2005) in this regard.

2.2.2 Incidents involving vehicles

Paragraph 11 of the 2008 Scheme now provides a definition of 'vehicle', when a vehicle is used to inflict injury deliberately. A vehicle is 'any device by which persons, animals or goods are or can be transported on or under land or water, or by air'. It would appear to the authors that this may include a fork-lift truck or even a shopping trolley! In the recent case of *Tait* v. *CICAP* [2009] EWHC 767 (Admin), a police officer was entitled to recover under the 2001 Scheme when his car was rammed by the driver of a stolen car, whose intention was to disable the police car rather than injure the officer, because it was a natural and probable consequence of his actions that the officer would be injured, and the driver could therefore be regarded as having intended to injure the officer. If a claim against a driver fails under the Scheme, it is worth checking whether an applicant has a claim against the driver's insurance company or the Motor Insurers' Bureau under the Uninsured or Untraced Drivers Agreements. Further details of this provision and other specific examples of eligible incidents are detailed in Chapter 2 of *Criminal Injuries Compensation Claims* (Law Society, 2005).

2.3 REDUCTION OR WITHHOLDING OF AWARDS

Paragraph 13 of the 2008 Scheme sets out the same basis for reducing awards as in the previous Schemes, such that: 'A claims officer *may* [our emphasis], withhold or reduce an award' where he or she considers that:

(a) the applicant failed to report the crime to the police or another authority;
(b) the applicant failed to cooperate with the police;
(c) the applicant failed to assist the CICA in connection with the application;
(d) the applicant's conduct before, during or after the incident makes a full award inappropriate; or
(e) the applicant's previous criminal convictions make a full or any award inappropriate.

A full discussion of these issues is contained in *Criminal Injuries Compensation Claims*, Chapters 5–7 and any changes to the previous provisions are detailed below.

2.3.1 Character of applicant

The use of the word 'may' in paragraph 13 implies that the matter remains one of discretion for the claims officer; however, a new paragraph has been inserted at paragraph 14(3), which says that:

> In considering the issue of character under paragraph 13(1)(e), a claims officer must withhold or reduce an award to reflect unspent criminal convictions unless he or she considers that there are exceptional reasons not to do so.

The 2008 Scheme Guide, at Section 2, paragraph 15 says 'The Scheme says we must reduce or refuse an award if you have a criminal record.' It is not clear what would amount to 'exceptional reasons'. It is arguable that if the injury suffered was very serious, it would be disproportionate to reduce or withhold an award in respect of fairly minor criminal convictions. Further, it may be argued that the 'exceptional reasons' exception should apply where the applicant's previous convictions were all drug-related and the applicant could show that he or she was now drug-free, and therefore should be treated as a rehabilitated or reformed character.

2.3.2 Penalty points system

The penalty points system remains the basis for calculating a reduction on the basis of criminal convictions, although neither the CICA nor the First-tier Tribunal are bound by that system and retain overall discretion. The penalty points system is simply the starting point for any reduction. Appendix 5 to the 2008 Scheme Guide sets out the relevant table for all applications made after 3 November 2008, which is set out below; it slightly refines the 2001 Scheme's table. (The basis for applying penalty points remained unchanged from the 2001 Scheme – see page 424 of *Criminal Injuries Compensation Claims* (Law Society, 2005) and Appendix 5 to the 2008 Scheme Guide). As Appendix 5, paragraph 4 to the 2008 Scheme Guide spells out: 'We will also take account of any convictions you receive after the incident or after applying, right through to the date when your case is finally settled'. Paragraph 6 goes on 'We are not bound by the penalty-points system, but we must take account of all unspent convictions. The penalty points are our starting point, but we consider convictions and penalty points together with all the other circumstances of the application.'

Penalty points	*Percentage reduction*
1	10%
2	15%
3	25%
4	30%
5	35%
6	50%
7	60%
8	70%
9	80%
10	100%

2.3.3 Conduct

A recent case *R. (on the application of Mohammed)* v. *CICAP* [2008] EWHC 1733 (Admin), considered paragraph 13(1)(d) in relation to conduct during an incident. In that case, an application on behalf of a man who had not walked away from a fight, but had waited outside an assailant's home and called for reinforcements, was refused, even though the man was killed by the assailant in the ensuing fight.

The immigration status of an applicant was considered under 'conduct' in *R. (on the application of Andronati)* v. *CICAP* [2006] EWHC 1420. The applicant was the victim of a rape. Both the CICA and the CICAP declined to make an award on the basis that the applicant was in the UK illegally, having overstayed her leave to remain. She was refused asylum in the UK but was then granted asylum in Ireland. The CICA rejected the claim on the basis of paragraph 13(e) of the 2001 Scheme, and the CICAP refused an appeal, finding that the applicant's conduct and character, under paragraph 13(d) and (e), in remaining in the UK unlawfully, made an award from public funds inappropriate. The applicant sought judicial review of that decision, and the court found that the CICAP had failed to consider the impact of the subsequent granting of asylum, and that the Panel should have considered whether the applicant could reasonably have been expected to leave the UK in circumstances when she had a well-founded fear of persecution.

2.3.4 Failing to respond to the CICA's communications

An additional ground for withholding an award has been included at paragraph 14(1) for situations where 'the applicant has repeatedly and without reasonable excuse' failed to respond to the CICA's communications at his or her last known address. This provision may be unduly harsh to those applicants who are unrepresented and live somewhat chaotic lives, perhaps because of their injuries. One can imagine applicants suffering from psychological or psychiatric injuries, who may omit to inform the CICA of a change of address, or who find it difficult to respond expediently to correspondence dealing with the application.

2.3.5 Family violence

Paragraph 17 of the 2008 Scheme reinforces the principle that an award will be withheld where the assailant lived with the victim, unless the assailant has since been prosecuted (or the claims officer is satisfied that there were good reasons why a prosecution was not brought) or unless the assailant stopped living with the victim before the application was made. Paragraph 17(2) clarifies that same sex couples and a man and woman living together as man and wife will be treated as members of the same family, whether or not they are married or civil partners within the meaning of that term in the Civil Partnership Act 2004.

PART 2 ASSESSMENT OF COMPENSATION

3 INJURY AWARDS

3.1 INTRODUCTION

As under the 1996 and 2001 Schemes, in accordance with the Criminal Injuries Compensation Act 1995, compensation under the 2008 Scheme is made up of a standard amount of compensation (commonly known as the tariff or injury award) plus an additional amount of compensation for loss of earnings and/or special expenses, if appropriate. Special provisions govern the award of additional compensation in fatal cases. Many of the provisions in the earlier Schemes remain unchanged and full details of all these possible types of compensation are detailed in Chapters 9–12 of *Criminal Injuries Compensation Claims* (Law Society, 2005). This book details any changes to those provisions in the 2008 Scheme. This chapter deals with the injury or tariff awards, **Chapter 4** covers claims for loss of earnings, **Chapter 5** covers claims for special expenses and deductions, and **Chapter 6** deals with fatal claims.

3.2 MAXIMUM AWARD UNDER 2008 SCHEME

As under the 2001 Scheme, the maximum award remains at £500,000 under the 2008 Scheme (paragraph 24), despite the arguments raised by victims' representatives that this limit has caused significant injustice to the most injured victims. The definition of the maximum award is also unchanged so that the cap is applied before any reduction under paragraphs 13–15 for lack of cooperation, conduct or character.

3.3 TARIFF AWARDS

The structure of the 2008 Scheme is the same as the 1996 and 2001 Schemes in that it provides for a tariff system, albeit with a new tariff. The tariff contains some changes although many levels of awards remain the same, with no increase to take account of inflation, despite the seven years since the previous levels were set. Concern remains amongst victims' representatives as to why the tariffs are not reviewed more regularly in the same way as the Judicial Studies Board Guidelines.

The 2008 tariff should be carefully consulted, and it is set out in full at the end of the Scheme, which may be found at **Appendix 1** to this book.

3.3.1 Notable changes in 2008 tariff

Psychiatric damage

A welcome addition is the recognition of psychiatric damage caused by sexual assaults, and additional level 17 and 18 awards have been included for such injury, although the damage must be regarded as 'permanently disabling' and must be confirmed by psychiatric prognosis. In addition, where non-consensual penetration of the vagina, anus or mouth has occurred and has resulted in serious internal bodily injury and severe mental illness to adult or child victims, the level of award has been increased to £44,000 from £33,000.

Brain injuries

The awards for brain injuries have been modified and increased, with a more detailed range of awards provided for, which would appear to better meet the victims' needs. As an example, the awards for moderate brain damage have increased from £16,000 under the 2001 Scheme, to three levels of awards between £27,000 and £82,000 under the 2008 Scheme. The cap remains at £250,000 for the most serious brain injury. Note 15 to the tariff provides:

> A brain injury can cause physical and/or mental damage, resulting in, for example, spasticity, loss of balance, incontinence, or impairment of concentration, memory, motivation or personality. It can also commonly cause epilepsy, to a greater or lesser extent. Where the cause of any injury is brain damage there will not be additional awards for separate injuries but the seriousness of the combined effects will be measured together.

Therefore in some cases applicants whose injuries had fallen into the middle to higher brackets under the 2001 Scheme (which were very wide) may obtain lower awards for similar injuries, because there will be no 'addition' under the multiple injuries formula for the subdural haematoma or the epilepsy which was also caused by the traumatic head injury.

Teeth

A common injury in crimes of violence is damage to the victim's teeth and the 2008 tariff has revised the 2001 tariff to provide more generous awards across the board. The award for the loss of one front tooth has risen from £1,750 to £3,300.

Hands

The tariff for the loss of a dominant hand or arm has increased from £44,000 to £55,000, although the loss of a non-dominant hand/arm is reduced to £33,000. The loss of both thumbs has been substantially increased from £33,000 to £55,000.

Internal injuries

Some inexplicable changes have been introduced to the individual tariffs. For example, the award for loss of a kidney has been dramatically reduced from £22,000 to £11,000, while there has been a 250 per cent increase in the award for loss of a spleen from £4,400 to £11,000.

Multiple minor injuries

Multiple minor injuries will be compensated in accordance with Note 12 to the tariff. The criteria remain unchanged from those in the 2001 Scheme and are strictly applied. There is no discretion. There must be three or more separate minor injuries, with the symptoms of at least one lasting for six weeks. If there have not been two visits to or by the doctor within the six-week period, the claim will fail. More serious minor injuries will be compensated as before with the tariff award for the most serious injury, and then 30 per cent and 15 per cent of the less serious injuries. (See paragraph 27 of the 2008 Scheme.)

3.3.2 Additional guidance notes

At Appendix 6 to the 2008 Scheme, additional notes are provided which say:

> 4. Where the tariff compensates for an operation the award includes provision for the normal operation scarring.
> 5. When a person suffers both a physical injury and a mental injury, and the tariff amount for the physical injury is higher than that for the mental injury, the applicant will be entitled only to the tariff amount for the physical injury.
>
>   When a person suffers both a physical injury and a mental injury, and the tariff amount for the mental injury is the same as or higher than that for the physical injury, the applicant will be entitled to awards for the separate injuries in accordance with paragraph 27 of the Scheme (the serious multiple injury formula).
>
>   When a person is a victim of a sexual offence and also suffers a mental injury, the applicant will be entitled only to whichever is the higher of the two tariff amounts.

4 COMPENSATION FOR LOSS OF EARNINGS

4.1 INTRODUCTION

As explained in **Chapter 3** of this book, as under the 1996 and 2001 Schemes, compensation under the 2008 Scheme is made up of a standard amount of compensation (the tariff or injury award) plus an additional amount of compensation for loss of earnings and/or special expenses, if appropriate. Special provisions also govern the award of additional compensation in fatal cases. Many of the provisions in the earlier Schemes remain unchanged and full details of all these possible types of compensation are detailed in Chapters 9–12 of *Criminal Injuries Compensation Claims* (Law Society, 2005). This book details any changes to those provisions in the 2008 Scheme. **Chapter 3** deals with the injury or tariff awards, this chapter covers claims for loss of earnings, **Chapter 5** covers claims for special expenses and deductions, and **Chapter 6** deals with fatal claims.

4.2 LOSS OF EARNINGS

Paragraphs 30–34 of the 2008 Scheme govern claims for loss of earnings or earning capacity. In November 2008 the then Principal Judge, Roger Goodier, issued a series of practice guidance notes which take the form of standard directions for the preparation of appeals. They are numbered CI-1 to CI-6 and copies can be found at **Appendix 4** to this book or online at **www.cicap.gov.gsi**. Practice guidance CI-1 is relevant to claims for financial loss including loss of earnings, earning capacity, special expenses, state benefits and pension payments. As under the previous 1996 and 2001 Schemes, any claim is subject to a cap on the level of loss of earnings claimed and a bar on any claim for loss of earnings or earning capacity for the first 28 weeks of any loss. Full details of these provisions are set out in *Criminal Injuries Compensation Claims*, Chapter 9.

4.2.1 Period of loss

The 28-week rule still applies, such that the applicant must have lost earnings or earning capacity for longer than 28 weeks as a result of the injury, before compensation for loss of earnings/earning capacity will be payable. In short, an applicant cannot recover any compensation if he or she was off work for 28 weeks or less. The basis for assessment of loss of earnings is the multiplicand/multiplier approach, and will be adjusted to take into account the tables set out at Note 3 to the 2008 Scheme. Table A converts an annual loss over a period of years into a lump sum payable at the beginning of that period, while tables B and C allow the multiplier to be adjusted to allow for accelerated receipt and life expectancy. As under the 2001 Scheme, paragraph 33 of the 2008 Scheme allows the claims officer to make 'such other lump sum' award if the multiplier or multiplicand approach is impracticable.

4.2.2 Making an application for loss of earnings or loss of earning capacity

The basis of the claim should be notified promptly to the CICA and the applicant must produce documents in support. A separate supplementary form called 'Unable to work for more than 28 weeks' should be completed if a loss of earnings claim is to be pursued. If self-employed, an applicant should produce three years of accounts; if employed, a year's pay slips are required. See practice guidance CI-1.

Usually if it is agreed that there is a loss of earnings claim, the CICA will produce its own schedule of losses. The applicant should also produce a schedule, and the format should follow the CICA's own system, by showing losses as credits and deductions as debits. The practice guidance CI-1 states at paragraph 7 that the appellant and the CICA will have sought to agree the financial loss claim on an arithmetical basis no later than two weeks before the hearing, and will inform the Tribunal of areas of disagreement between them. Whilst this was fairly common practice previously, in the authors' experience it was certainly not done as a matter of course. Under the 2008 Scheme, practitioners should ensure they do what they can to comply with this process, as paragraph 8 of the same practice guidance states:

> An Appellant who fails to comply with this direction [i.e. all of CI-1] risks having the claim for financial loss struck out either in full or in part, and/or having an award withheld or reduced under paragraph 13(c) of the Scheme for failing to give reasonable assistance in connection with the application.

4.2.3 Cap on loss of earnings claim

The cap on loss of earnings is 1.5 times the median gross weekly earnings at the time of the assessment, and as at November 2008, practice guidance CI-4 set out that the then correct figure was £718.50 per week (£37,362 per annum). As at February 2010, that figure stands at £733.50 per week, or £38,142 per annum based on the 2009 Annual Survey of Hours and Earnings.

4.2.4 Further guidance

Section 3, paragraphs 29–33 of the 2008 Scheme Guide provides additional information on loss of earnings claims, as does Appendix 4 to the 2008 Scheme Guide. Paragraphs 3–6 of Appendix 4 state:

3. You are only eligible to claim loss of earnings if your inability to work is as a direct result of a criminal injury for which we have agreed a tariff payment, and not entirely or partly from other things, such as:
   - health problems before the injury, including mental health issues;
   - health problems which arose after the injury but which were not caused by the incident;
   - a previous injury or illness (caused perhaps by sport or an accident at work);
   - the financial insecurity of your type of work; or
   - you are self-employed, or have trading or cash-flow problems not connected with the injury.
4. You may be eligible for a payment towards:
   - what you have already lost (past loss of earnings); and
   - what you may lose as a result of not being able to return to work (future loss of earnings).
5. If we find you have been earning money without paying taxes or dishonestly receiving state benefits, we are likely to take this into account when considering your application.
6. If we have given you any interim payments we *will* [our emphasis] ask for these back.

There has always been an inherent power to ask for interim payments back. However, the authors have not encountered this being done in practice. It remains to be seen whether the policy will change under the 2008 Scheme having regard to the wording above. In so far as we are aware, the previous Chairman's guidance given in 2004 with regard to the exclusion of loss of earnings claims where there has been a failure to pay income tax still stands (see paragraph 9.4.5 of *Criminal Injuries Compensation Claims* (Law Society, 2005)). However, this is a 'conduct' issue under paragraph 13(d) or (e), so the entire claim may fail or be discounted across the board depending on the scale of the fraud. In the authors' experience, if the evidence demonstrates a failure to declare income over anything more than a *de minimis* period, and certainly if there is evidence of benefit fraud in addition, the appellant should actively consider abandoning his or her loss of earnings and loss of earning capacity claim prior to the appeal and restricting the claim to the tariff award and other special expenses.

As to future earnings, paragraph 13 of Appendix 4 to the 2008 Scheme Guide makes it clear that:

> We do not just compare your earnings before and after your injury. We have to look at your total income, including the sick pay you get from your employer, social security benefits, ill-health/injury pension and income from any other employment. We also take account of benefits you are entitled to. The Scheme says that if you could get any social security or other state benefits, we may delay making an award until you have taken steps to claim them.

Paragraph 14 of Appendix 4 adds:

> We also have to reduce any award we make for your lost earnings if you have received payment for this from an insurance policy which someone else (such as your

employer) paid for or contributed to. If you get payment for lost earnings from an insurance policy which you paid for yourself, we do not reduce your award.

4.3 LOSS OF PENSION

The basic rules for loss of pension as described in *Criminal Injuries Compensation Claims*, Chapter 9, remain unchanged. Therefore, the general rule remains that the CICA will compare like with like. Hence, in assessing the pension loss after normal retirement age the CICA will compare the anticipated occupational pension as against 100 per cent of the taxed value of ill health and injury pensions plus any state benefits which the applicant will continue to receive. The real issue which arises under the 2008 Scheme in respect of loss of pension claims is the manner in which and the period over which deductions are to be made and this is considered in detail below in **Chapter 5**.

5 SPECIAL EXPENSES AND DEDUCTIONS

5.1 INTRODUCTION

As explained in **Chapters** 3 and 4, compensation under the 2008 Scheme is made up of a standard amount of compensation (the tariff or injury award) plus an additional amount of compensation for loss of earnings and/or special expenses, if appropriate. Special provisions also govern the award of additional compensation in fatal cases. Many of the provisions in the earlier Schemes remain unchanged and full details of all these possible types of compensation are detailed in Chapters 9–12 of *Criminal Injuries Compensation Claims* (Law Society, 2005). This book details any changes to those provisions in the 2008 Scheme. **Chapter 3** deals with the injury or tariff awards, **Chapter 4** covers claims for loss of earnings, this chapter covers claims for special expenses and deductions, and **Chapter 6** deals with fatal claims.

5.2 SPECIAL EXPENSES

The provisions for special expenses are set out in paragraphs 35 and 36 of the 2008 Scheme.

5.2.1 The '28-week rule' for special expenses

As with the 2001 Scheme, the '28-week rule' remains, such that recoverability of any special expenses or care costs is subject to the applicant having lost earnings or earning capacity for 28 weeks or more. The compensation for special expenses and care costs is then backdated to the date of the injury.

5.2.2 Further guidance

Chapter 10 of *Criminal Injuries Compensation Claims* (Law Society, 2005) deals comprehensively with special expenses, and much of that chapter still applies to the 2008 Scheme. Paragraphs 24–35 of Appendix 4 to the 2008 Scheme Guide also provide useful information on special expenses in relation to the 2008 Scheme.

5.2.3 Care claims

The key change in the 2008 Scheme relates to care claims. Historically the CICA has approached claims on the basis that the only recoverable care costs are the costs directed at the applicant, rather than, for example, care to assist in caring for the applicant's children. In so doing, the CICA relied on the so-called 'Archer amendment' and its own view of 'core care'. The amended definition of care pursuant to the 2008 Scheme is at paragraph 35(d)(iii):

> care (in connection with the applicant's bodily functions or the preparation of meals) and supervision (to avoid substantial danger to the applicant or others), whether in a residential establishment or at home, which is not provided or available free of charge from the National Health Service, local authorities or any other agency, provided that a claims officer considers such expense to be necessary as a direct consequence of the injury

This appears to be a further tightening of the definition of care and mirrors the wording used in assessing claims for the care element of the Disability Living Allowance. If a care report has been commissioned, the nursing expert ought to have this definition firmly in mind because it is plainly so different from the common law approach. It is clear that matters relating to personal hygiene, dressing, taking medication and feeding the applicant will all still be covered.

5.2.4 Claims for supervision

The 'supervision (to avoid substantial danger to the applicant or others)' element, is less straightforward. Under the 2001 Scheme, an applicant was successful in recovering care costs in the following circumstances. She had been suffering severe post-traumatic stress disorder, having witnessed her brother being brutally murdered, and had also developed severe agoraphobia. The prognosis was for eventual recovery over a period of four years provided she had regular support to assist her in attending counselling and cognitive behavioural therapy (CBT) appointments and to ensure she took gradual steps to getting back into a normal routine. She was awarded time-limited care costs to cover the cost of family members or paid 'buddies' to enable her to go out and attend appointments and CBT and to try to get back to a normal life. Under the 2008 Scheme, it would seem that she would fail the 'substantial danger to herself or others' test.

There are many brain damaged applicants, or those with psychiatric injuries, who pose no danger to themselves or others, but have limited confidence and do not feel safe to go out unaccompanied, and in those circumstances a carer or buddy is their lifeline. They are likely to suffer as a consequence of this amendment. If the applicant suffers from aggression or disinhibition, this may be sufficient to overcome the 'danger' hurdle. Although there has been no change in the provision for gratuitous care (now at paragraph 35(2)) such a claim will now have to be considered with the care definition in paragraph 35(1) in mind. A family member's time will only be compensated where it covers the bodily functions, preparation of meals and 'danger to the applicant or others' test. If you are able to overcome the new test, the CICA is likely in our experience to accept the rates set out in the

Professional Negligence Bar Association's *Facts and Figures Tables for the Calculation of Damages* (Sweet & Maxwell, updated annually) with a 25 per cent discount.

5.2.5 Provision of NHS or local authority care or accommodation

In serious injury cases, a question often arises, in both common law cases and cases involving the CICA, as to whether care will continue to be provided to the applicant by the National Health Service or local authorities (see paragraph 35(1)(d)(iii)) free of charge. Chapter 10 of *Criminal Injuries Compensation Claims* considers this issue although the law has moved on as discussed below. The NHS and local authorities often decline to guarantee that they will continue to provide care, such that it is unclear whether there will be a cost to the applicant in the future. Three recent authorities consider the issue further:

- *Peters* v. *East Midlands Strategic Heath Authority* [2009] EWCA Civ 145;
- *R (on the application of B)* v. *CICAP* [2007] EWHC 180 (QB);
- *Crofton* v. *NHSLA* [2007] EWCA Civ 71.

It is not possible to consider this topic in detail in this book, but these cases examine the complexities of local authority powers under National Assistance Act 1948, ss.21(1), 24(3) and 29 and the general conclusion is that this is a legal minefield crying out for reform. Butterfield J in the first instance decision in *Peters* concluded that 'a mere reading of this tortuous analysis of the labyrinthine legislative provisions is sufficient to persuade me to add my name to the roll call of those who have condemned these regulations as being obscure, opaque and convoluted'.

In *Peters* the court found that the claimant was entitled to be privately self-funded and that provided the risk of double recovery could be avoided, she was entitled to seek the entire costs of her future care from the tortfeasor. The Court of Appeal got around the double recovery issue by the Deputy giving an undertaking not to seek local authority accommodation or care under the Court of Protection order.

Thus, in cases where there is a tortfeasor, the claimant may rely on the tortfeasor for the funding of care costs, provided the risk of double recovery is avoided. What is the situation though in statutory Scheme cases where there is no tortfeasor? In *R (on the application of B)* the applicant recovered the cost of care from the CICA following the reasoning in the common law cases despite the absence of a tortfeasor. However, *R (on the application of B)* was a 1990 Scheme case which followed common law principles. Any outstanding 1990 Scheme cases can therefore expect the reasoning in *Peters* to be followed.

There do not seem to be any reported cases relating to this issue being dealt with under the 1996, 2001 or 2008 Schemes, as yet. It is likely that the CICA will take a different approach under those Schemes given the absence of a tortfeasor and the overriding desire to protect the public purse. On 21 May 2009, the First-tier Tribunal determined the case of Stephen Palfrey, the facts of which are as follows. The appellant was in full-time local authority residential care as a result of serious brain injuries. He required 24-hour care and supervision. He had been in the same unit for three years prior to the hearing. His position appeared to be relatively stable there but he was a long way from family members and the local authority could not give any guarantees as to future funding. His situation was reviewed annually. The Tribunal took the view that the reality was that there would be continued local authority provision of some sort into the future. The appellant was in his 30s and had a normal life expectancy. The Tribunal did not accept that there was a significant risk that all funding would cease in the future such that the appellant would be left without residential care. It found that there was a 25 per cent chance of his future funding being deficient, such that a top-up of care would be required to meet his reasonable needs and that the degree of deficiency was likely to be no less than 25 per cent. The annual cost of care was agreed at £104,000. The Tribunal awarded a sum of £75,000 which represented £104,000 × life multiplier × 25% × 25% to reflect the adverse contingencies in respect of future local authority provision. This approach is one which may be considered just in principle given the absence of a privately insured tortfeasor and the need to protect the public purse. However, it does pose difficult questions. How does one assess the degree of the risk and the magnitude of it and the period over which it might manifest? The history of an individual case will be relevant and if there has been deficient provision, uncertainty regarding provision or there is change predicted on the horizon the appellant may be able to make the case for a higher award for this contingency.

The Tribunal is likely to take account of all the circumstances of each case. It should consider what has been provided by the local authority or primary care trust to date, with a view to assessing the likely provision of care in the future. Evidence from the local authority regarding provision of future care and funding should be obtained. If the funding cannot be guaranteed beyond a certain date, it may be that the whole cost of the care after that date could be recovered, or a percentage of it to reflect the fact that some provision would continue to be made by the local authority in any event, but there would be a shortfall.

5.2.6 Top-up claims and case management

The CICA has accepted top-up care claims historically under the 1996 and 2001 Schemes, whereby the CICA accepted that the local authority provision was inadequate such that a top-up gratuitous care provision was allowed. For example, where the residential costs of the applicant's care are being met by the local authority or NHS but there is no provision for the applicant to be escorted out of the residential unit, to attend classes, or visit family, a top-up allowance may be allowed. With the new 'care' definition under the 2008 Scheme, such a claim may become increasingly difficult, but it should be considered. Claims for the costs of case management have hitherto been recoverable in suitable cases as a component of the care costs of the applicant, though the CICA will frequently challenge the need for this. Under the 2008 Scheme, the definition of care is so tight that it remains to be seen if case management costs will be recoverable. It may be that one can argue that these form 'other costs associated with the administration of the applicant's affairs due to his or her lack of mental capacity (such as the costs of administering a power of attorney, the fees of a receiver or deputy appointed to act in a professional capacity [...] provided that the claims officer considers that the costs were necessarily incurred as a result of the injury and are reasonable'. See paragraph 35(f) of the 2008 Scheme.

5.2.7 Claims for special equipment

Paragraph 36(2) of the 2008 Scheme provides a new addition in relation to special equipment:

> Where, at the time the claim is assessed, a claims officer is satisfied that the need for special equipment is likely to continue and that the equipment will require replacement on occasions in the future, the claims officer will calculate the replacement value at each date of replacement, being the cost of the new equipment less the sale value of the old equipment and select an appropriate discount factor in accordance with paragraph 32 [...] taking account of any other factors and contingencies which appear to him or her to be relevant.

It is difficult to see how a claims officer will be able to value, at an assessment in 2010, the sale value of an old wheelchair in say 2016. 'Salvage' value may have been a more appropriate term, as it seems that if special equipment is deemed to have a limited lifespan one would imagine that the sale value of the used item would be very modest indeed. In order to avoid this being unfair to an applicant, it may be that providers of specialist equipment could be asked for their views as to salvage or sale value of old equipment, to assist applicants in drafting a schedule.

Appendix 4 to the 2008 Scheme Guide considers special equipment and expenses at paragraphs 31–31. Paragraph 31 stresses that the CICA will only pay for items that are not available free of charge from the local authority, NHS or other agency.

5.2.8 Costs of administration of affairs

Paragraph 35(1) of the 2008 Scheme makes additional changes in relation to the costs associated with the administration of the affairs of applicants with mental incapacity. These changes are welcome in that they expressly permit the recovery of:

- costs payable to the Public Guardian or Court of Protection, or Sheriff Court (paragraph 35(1)(e));
- other costs associated with the administration of the applicant's affairs due to his or her lack of mental capacity (paragraph 35(1)(f));
- the reasonable cost of setting up and administering a trust pursuant to a direction given by the claims officer under paragraph 50 (paragraph 35(1)(g)).

Significantly, and very much in favour of applicants, paragraph 13(2) of the Scheme contains a new provision which states: 'No amount awarded in accordance with paragraph 35(1)(e),(f), or (g) (expenses associated with lack of mental capacity or trusts) will be reduced under sub-paragraph (1) above or under paragraph 14, unless the whole award is withheld under those provisions.' Therefore, whereas prior to the 2008 Scheme a percentage reduction would bite on every head of loss including the recoverable costs of the Court of Protection, now this head of loss will be ring fenced.

5.2.9 Mental incapacity

Chapter 21 of *Criminal Injuries Compensation Claims*, at paragraph 21.3, dealt in some detail with the provisions relating to the administration of awards including situations whereby the victim did not have capacity under the Mental Health Act 1983. Practitioners should note that the law relating to capacity has been substantially overhauled now pursuant to the Mental Capacity Act 2005 which came into force on 1 October 2007. The Act is supported by practical guidance in the form of a Code of Practice which runs to over 300 pages. Persons acting in a professional capacity (defined in s.42(4) and (5)) have a duty to follow the Code of Practice. This can be obtained from the website for the Office of the Public Guardian (OPG) at **www.publicguardian.gov.uk**. Generally speaking, the Act applies to all persons over the age of 18 and, subject to three minor instances, persons aged 16 and 17. It only applies to persons under 16 in so far as the Scheme is likely to be concerned where the individual is likely to lack capacity to make financial decisions when they reach the age of 18 (see s.18(3)). The Act has five key principles.

1. A person must be assumed to have capacity unless it is established that he or she lacks capacity.
2. A person is not to be treated as unable to make a decision unless all practicable steps to help him or her to do so have been taken without success.
3. A person is not to be treated as unable to make a decision merely because he or she makes an unwise decision.
4. An act done, or decision made, under the Act for or on behalf of a person who lacks capacity must be done, or made, in his or her 'best interests'.
5. Before the act is done, or the decision is made, regard must be had to whether the purpose for which it is needed can be effectively achieved in a way that is less restrictive of the person's rights and freedom of action.

Section 2 defines the lack of capacity in relation to a matter if at the material time he or she is 'unable to make a decision for himself in relation to the matter because of an impairment of, or a disturbance in the functioning of, the mind or brain'. This can be permanent or temporary and cannot be established merely by reference to a person's age or appearance or his or her condition, or an aspect of his or her behaviour which might lead others to make unjustified assumptions about his or her incapacity. In making the assessment under s.2, further considerations as listed under s.3 must be applied. In cases of doubt about capacity or in cases where the Court of Protection may need to be involved, a formal assessment and doctor's opinion ought to be sought (paragraph 4.54 of the Code). It is worthy of note that the Code of Practice rather suggests that the Act's definition is in line with existing common law tests although it is said: 'judges can adopt the new definition if they think it is appropriate' (paragraph 4.33). It is beyond the remit of this work to consider the Act further. Practitioners will find a copy of the Act at **www.opsi.gov.uk** and other useful information on the OPG's website at **www.publicguardian.gov.uk**.

5.3 DEDUCTIONS

Paragraphs 45–49 of the 2008 Scheme provide for the effect on awards of benefits or insurance payments. Chapter 11 of *Criminal Injuries Compensation Claims* covers this topic in considerable detail. This section of the book will focus on the limited changes brought about by the 2008 Scheme.

5.3.1 Social security benefits and insurance payments

Whilst paragraph 45 of the 2008 Scheme has been re-worded, the substance remains the same, in that social security benefits and insurance payments (other than those privately funded by the applicant or his or her parent if under 18 at the time of the injury) all have to be deducted from compensation for the same contingency. In other words, Income Support benefits will be deducted from loss of earnings and Disability Living Allowance will be deducted from the care claim. If the claimant's self-funded insurance policy pays out damages for special equipment or private treatment, credit must be given for those sums, but any compensation for the injury is ignored as is any insurance that compensates the claimant for lost earnings.

5.3.2 Acceleration cases

The 2008 Scheme has made one key change in respect of loss of earnings and relevant deductions. In the case of *R. (on the application of Vick)* v. *CICAP* [2005] EWHC 1575, a claim made under the 2001 Scheme, the applicant police officer had suffered loss of earnings amounting to about £40,000 as a result of a criminal injury which was described as an acceleration injury (that is, the symptoms of the injury were only attributable to the incident for a limited period as a result of pre-existing problems). The case took a number of years to reach the assessment stage, and by the time of the assessment, the applicant was actually £3,700 per annum better off as a result of enhanced benefits he received after the age of 55. The applicant argued that paragraph 31 of the 2001 Scheme, and paragraphs 47 (deductions for pensions) and 48 (deduction of present or future payments made on account of the injury) did not allow the future benefits to be set off against the past losses. He argued successfully that, as the losses had already ceased at the date of assessment, there was no loss post-dating the assessment, thus there was no deduction to be made.

Under the 2008 Scheme, the relevant paragraphs have been amended to rule out the option of this argument. Paragraph 45(3) of the 2008 Scheme provides that:

> a reduction under this paragraph will be made irrespective of the period in respect of which the social security benefits or insurance payments have been, or will be paid.

> In particular, the reduction will be made whether or not any actual loss occurred or will occur in that period.

This would appear to fall in line with the general approach of the Schemes, that credit must be given for any benefits or payments which have arisen or will arise in the future, provided they are consequent upon the injury.

5.3.3 Deduction of pension payments

Pension payments remain deductible under paragraph 46 of the 2008 Scheme (unless paid for fully by the victim or a dependant). As under the 2001 Scheme, where taxable, if a pension is being paid prior to the applicant's normal retirement age because of the criminal injury, one half of the gross value of the pension is deducted from the loss of earnings claim, otherwise the pension payments will be deducted in full. When assessing the loss of pension from normal retirement age, as set out in 4.3 above, 100 per cent of the taxed (if taxable) or full value of any pension being paid will be deducted from the pension loss claim. Injury gratuity awards (usually from employers' insurance policies) are still to be deducted in full against loss of earnings. Any compensation awarded by a civil court, or a criminal court, or by means of any other settlement, must be deducted. Although such awards are relatively rare in practice, paragraph 48(3) now states that a claims officer may decline to process an application further until the applicant has shown that he or she has exhausted all options to obtain damages or compensation through other means. The authors think this relates to cases where it is apparent to the CICA that the applicant has a civil claim pending. The application form for 2008 Scheme claims states that the applicant will give 'details of claims for compensation or damages related to the injury set out in this form from any other person or organisation, and I understand that you can delay settling my claim while this is resolved'. This puts on a more formal footing the previous practice of the CICA to hold a claim under the Scheme in abeyance pending the resolution one way or the other of a civil claim.

6 COMPENSATION IN FATAL CASES

6.1 INTRODUCTION

As explained in the previous chapters of this book, compensation under the 2008 Scheme is normally made up of a standard amount of compensation (the tariff or injury award) plus an additional amount of compensation for loss of earnings and/or special expenses, if appropriate. However, special provisions govern the award of additional compensation in fatal cases. Many of the provisions in the earlier Schemes remain unchanged and full details of all the provisions relating to fatal cases are set out in Chapter 12 of *Criminal Injuries Compensation Claims* (Law Society, 2005). This chapter of the book details any changes to those provisions in the 2008 Scheme.

6.2 FATAL CLAIMS

Paragraphs 37–44 of the 2008 Scheme cover fatal claims and the provisions remain broadly unchanged from the provisions in the 1996 and 2001 Schemes.

6.2.1 Claim by estate for funeral expenses.

The basis for claiming funeral expenses remains unchanged. Whoever paid for the funeral can claim funeral expenses, even if the person paying has a criminal record. The victim's conduct and character will be considered and may result in the claim for funeral expenses being reduced or disallowed. Where the victim has died in consequence of the injury, the only loss recoverable on behalf of the estate is the cost of funeral expenses. Where the deceased was a victim of a criminal injury but had not received an award before dying of unrelated causes, the claim for special expenses and loss of earnings can still be pursued by a qualifying claimant who was dependent upon the victim.

6.2.2 Qualifying claimants

The definition of a 'qualifying claimant' remains largely unchanged and includes spouse/former spouse, cohabitee, same sex partner, parents and children. It is now clarified that where ill health or infirmity prevented the deceased and the qualifying claimant from living together this does not disqualify the claimant (paragraph 38(2)(a)). Appendix 3 to the 2008 Scheme Guide provides additional guidance. The definition of child is not limited to a person below the age of 18. It includes adult children and an unborn child of the person who has died, who was born alive after the victim died.

6.2.3 Bereavement award

Paragraph 39 provides for a bereavement award to be paid to a qualifying claimant, although former/estranged spouses or civil partners are excluded from this element of compensation. The award for one qualifying claimant is £11,000 under the 2008 Scheme, while if there is more than one qualifying claimant the level for each claimant is £5,500. Unlike in common law claims, the parents of a victim can recover compensation whatever the age of the victim.

6.2.4 Additional compensation

If the qualifying claimant was financially dependent upon the deceased, compensation may be payable, save that if the deceased's income was from benefits only, no dependency will be established. The basis for the dependency calculation is the same as under paragraphs 31–35 of the Scheme save that where the deceased had been living with the qualifying claimant, the claims officer will make a proportional reduction to take account of the deceased's own expenses. Paragraph 42 retains the provision that a child can seek the loss of parental services at an annual rate of £2,000, with an appropriate multiplier up to age 18. This is clearly a very modest rate for the loss of parental services, and it is notable that the rate has been static for 12 years now. The total cap of £500,000 remains, such that the amount payable to the victim and the qualifying claimant(s) will not exceed that sum.

6.3 DEDUCTIONS

Paragraph 45 of the 2008 Scheme has been amended to mirror the changes detailed at **5.3.2** above, triggered by the decision in *R. (on the application of Vick)* v. *CICAP* [2005] EWHC 1575. The net effect is as stated at paragraph 45(3) and (4):

> (3) Subject to sub-paragraph (4) below, a reduction under this paragraph will be made irrespective of the period in respect of which the social security benefits or insurance payments have been, or will be paid. In particular, the reduction will be made whether or not any actual loss occurred or will occur in that period.
>
> (4) No reduction under this paragraph will be made to take account of any social security benefits or insurance payments paid in respect of the first 28 weeks of lost earnings.

Details of the provisions of the 2008 Scheme relating to the deductions that may have to be made from any fatal claim for compensation are outlined in **Chapter 5**.

PART 3 **PROCEDURE**

7 MAKING APPLICATIONS UNDER THE 2008 SCHEME

7.1 INTRODUCTION

The broad jurisdictional and geographical boundaries governing applications for compensation under the 2008 Scheme have remained largely unchanged from those applicable under the 1996 and 2001 Schemes and many of the procedures for making an application and the consideration of that application by the CICA remain the same. Full details of all these unchanged provisions and detailed advice on many aspects of making a claim and gathering and presenting evidence in support of such a claim are set out in Part 3, Chapters 13–21 of *Criminal Injuries Compensation Claims* (Law Society, 2005) and are beyond the scope of this book. This book primarily details any changes to those provisions in the 2008 Scheme. This chapter deals with the making of an application to the CICA, **Chapter 8** deals with reviews of decisions, **Chapter 9** deals with reconsideration and re-opening of final decisions, **Chapter 10** deals with appeals, and **Chapter 11** deals with the rules.

7.2 ADMINISTRATION OF THE SCHEME

Paragraphs 2–5 of the 2008 Scheme provide for the administration of the Scheme. Claims officers will decide upon applications lodged, and will determine in accordance with the 2008 Scheme what awards, if any, should be made, and how they should be paid. Any appeal against their decision will be to the First-tier Tribunal.

7.3 TIME LIMIT FOR MAKING AN APPLICATION

Any application for compensation must be made within two years from the date of the incident giving rise to the injury. The claims officer's discretion for waiving that time limit has been reduced. Under the 2001 Scheme, a claims officer could waive the time limit:

> where he considers that, by reason of the particular circumstances of the case, it is reasonable and in the interests of justice to do so.

Under the 2008 Scheme, paragraph 18, a claims officer can only now waive the time limit, where:

he or she considers that:

(a) it is practicable for the application to be considered; and
(b) in the particular circumstances of the case, it would not have been reasonable to expect the applicant to have made an application within the two-year period.

Both parts of the test must be met. It is crucial that an applicant provides as much evidence as possible at the outset to ensure that the 'practicability' hurdle can be overcome. The 2008 Scheme Guide suggests at Appendix 2, paragraph 5, that the time limit may be waived where a person was sexually abused as a child, but could not report the abuse until they became an adult. However, the Guide adds: 'we would expect that the person reports the abuse as soon as it is reasonable for them to do so'. It is not clear how this will be applied in practice, but it appears to be a stricter test than the 2001 test. Paragraph 19 of the 2008 Scheme establishes that it is for the applicant to prove the justification for waiver.

7.4 CASE MANAGEMENT

Case management is governed by paragraph 20 of the 2008 Scheme, which directs that the claims officer may make appropriate directions, and impose conditions, if required, and the requisite standard of proof in all matters is the 'balance of probabilities'. If the claims officer considers that an examination of the injury is required, the CICA will arrange for a medical examination and will meet the reasonable expenses of the applicant incurred in connection with that. Note that paragraph 19(2) provides that if the applicant incurs a fee for a medical report (or other ancillary expenses) to assist in making his or her claim, the CICA is not liable for those expenses unless the claims officer considers it is reasonable for the CICA to meet them in full or in part. Thus, where the CICA has failed to instruct an appropriate expert, the applicant can then identify an expert and invite the CICA to agree to the instruction and to meet the costs of such report. Practice statement CI-3 supplements paragraph 19(2) and is located at **Appendix 4** to this book. It should be noted though that rule 10 of the Tribunal Procedure Rules (see **Chapters 10** and **11**) provides that there is no general power to award costs, so the costs provision is limited to the issue of experts' costs.

7.4.1 Public funding for CICA claims

At paragraph 14.6.6 of *Criminal Injuries Compensation Claims* (Law Society, 2005), it was stated that there is no public funding for these claims save that in some circumstances legal aid can be obtained in respect of judicial review applications. This statement was incorrect and the authors wish to apologise for this error. In fact, there continues to be some limited public funding assistance available under the old 'Green Form' Scheme, which covers preparatory work only and not hearings.

7.5 DETERMINATION OF APPLICATIONS AND PAYMENT OF AWARDS

Paragraphs 50–52 concern the determination of applications and payment of awards under the 2008 Scheme. These paragraphs replicate those contained in the 2001 Scheme save for the following addition. Paragraph 50(1) now requires that:

> Written acceptance of an award must be received by the Authority within 90 days of the date the decision was issued. If such an acceptance is not received within that period, and no application for a review under paragraph 59 has been made, the Authority may withdraw the award.

However, a claims officer may extend the time limit, whether or not it has already expired, if the applicant has made a written request for an extension and the claims officer considers that there are exceptional circumstances which justify the granting of an extension. Again, it remains to be seen what will amount to exceptional circumstances, such as to justify a time extension, but it is likely that where serious injuries are involved, an extension will be allowed. As a general rule, a written application for an extension of time should be made as soon as possible.

7.6 TRUST COSTS

It should be noted that if the claims officer directs that a trust should be set up to administer an award, the reasonable costs of setting up and running that trust can be recovered pursuant to paragraph 35 of the 2008 Scheme. See further 5.2.8 and 5.2.9 above in relation to the administration of awards and mental incapacity. See also Chapter 21 of *Criminal Injuries Compensation Claims* (Law Society, 2005) which deals generally with the administration of awards.

8 REVIEW OF DECISIONS

8.1 INTRODUCTION

This chapter covers the provisions in the 2008 Scheme relating to seeking a review of a decision by the CICA. This topic was covered in detail in Chapter 15 of *Criminal Injuries Compensation Claims* (Law Society, 2005) and many of the provisions remain largely unchanged from the provisions in the 2001 Scheme. There are, however, a few significant changes and this chapter outlines the procedural position under the 2008 Scheme.

8.2 GROUNDS FOR A REVIEW

If an applicant is dissatisfied with the decision by a claims officer he or she may, pursuant to paragraph 58 of the 2008 Scheme, seek a review when notification of the decision is made. The basic procedural position remains unchanged from the 2001 Scheme but there are some inconsequential updating and clarifying amendments to paragraph 58 which now reads:

> (1) An applicant may seek a review of any decision under this Scheme by a claims officer:
>
> (a) not to waive or extend the time limit in paragraph 18 (application for compensation) or paragraph 59 (application for review); or
> (b) not to re-open a case under paragraphs 56-57; or
> (c) to withhold an award, including such decision made on reconsideration of an award under paragraphs 53-54; or
> (d) to make an award, including a decision to make a reduced award whether or not on reconsideration of an award under paragraphs 53-54; or
> (e) to require repayment of an award under paragraph 49; or
> (f) to withdraw an award under paragraph 50(1).
>
> (2) An applicant may not, however, seek the review of any such decision:
>
> (a) where the decision was itself made on a review under paragraph 60 and either the applicant did not appeal against it or the appeal did not result in a direction from the First-tier Tribunal; or
> (b) where the decision was made in accordance with a direction by the First-tier Tribunal on determining an appeal under paragraph 64.

The applicant may, therefore, appeal any decision of the claims officer except where the decision itself is a review decision, or where it is a decision made after an appeal under paragraph 64.

8.2.1 Merits of applying for a review

The CICA publishes a leaflet 'Asking for a Review' which can be obtained on its website: **www.cica.gov.uk**. The leaflet states that the applicant should apply for a review where:

- you think our decision was wrong;
- you think we have not taken account of all the relevant information;
- you think we have looked at the wrong information; or
- you have any further information you would like us to consider.

In the authors' experience in many cases there is much to be gained by seeking a review, especially if further medical or witness evidence may be available or should be obtained to complete the picture. Generally speaking it will cost virtually nothing to proceed to a review, save where the CICA disagrees with the need for ancillary medical evidence or the need for further enquiries and the applicant is left to fund these at his or her discretion (see in this regard the Court of Appeal's decision in *C (A Child)* v. *Secretary of State for the Home Department* [2004] EWCA Civ 234 and paragraph 21 of the Scheme which deal with the duty of the CICA to perform 'an examination of the injury'). However, caution should be exercised since there will be times when an initial decision may be generous within the usual application of the Scheme and a potentially adverse point may have been given less weight by one claims officer and may be given more weight by another claims officer. It remains the position that the claims officer will not be bound by the earlier decision and the review decision may be more or less favourable or the same so far as the applicant is concerned.

8.3 TIME LIMIT AND FORM OF APPLICATION

Pursuant to paragraph 59 of the 2008 Scheme the time limit remains unchanged at 90 days from the date of the decision, save that the wording has been refined to say 90 days from the date when the decision was 'issued'. The CICA's leaflet about reviews referred to above says that the application for the review must be received within 90 days of the date of their decision letter. If there has been some difficulty with the post or the decision arrives long after the date of the decision letter or if more time is required to obtain disclosure from the CICA and decide what further evidence is required, then consideration should be given to whether an extension of time should be sought. An extension of the time limit may be requested within the 90 days or retrospectively. (This differs from the position under the 2001 Scheme where on a strict reading retrospective applications for extension could not be granted.) However, under the 2008 Scheme, the request must be made in writing and will only be permitted where the claims officer considers that there are exceptional circumstances which justify the granting of an extension (paragraph 59(b)). The 2008 Scheme Guide (section 5, paragraph 3) says that:

> We will not accept any new evidence after the 90 days unless we have given you an extension. We will do this if it was not reasonable to have expected you to have made the request within the time limit. If this is the case, you will need to write to us. You can ask for an extension even after the 90 days have passed but we will only grant this if there are exceptional circumstances.

There is a slight anomaly here. The wording of paragraph 59 is fairly clear that whether or not the application for an extension is made within time it will only be granted where there are exceptional circumstances. Yet the 2008 Scheme Guide rather suggests that *if* the request was made *within* the 90 days *and* the evidence could *not reasonably* be obtained within that period then it will still be considered. Whereas, if the application is made outside the 90 days and the evidence therefore must follow beyond the 90-day limit, it will only be considered if there are exceptional circumstances. Our understanding of the day-to-day implementation of this rule and the guidance is that applications made for extensions or requests for review made within the 90-day limit giving a realistic and reasoned timescale for evidence to follow are generally regarded as acceptable by the CICA. By contrast, applications made retrospectively are permitted only when there are adjudged to be exceptional circumstances.

8.3.1 Form of application for a review

The application must be made in writing and can be done by way of a letter or on a pro forma form obtained from the CICA. The application should, according to the CICA's leaflet:

- tell us why you think the decision is wrong; and
- send with your form any further information you want us to consider.

Specific attention should be paid to the reasons given and any possible evidence which may be available to deal with these issues since the review application will be the focus for any further enquiries made by the CICA. As set out above, if the CICA does not agree to follow a certain line of enquiry or is satisfied with the evidence obtained to date, the applicant has a free hand to put before the CICA any evidence he or she may obtain. Tactically and having regard to the difficulties of funding these claims many practitioners adopt a 'wait and see' attitude towards the further evidence obtained by the CICA and take a final view at the appeal stage about the funding of further medical reports or obtaining other specialist expensive evidence. The advantage of this approach is that if the parties have reached an impasse about the way forward with evidence, an application can be made to the First-tier Tribunal for directions. (See **Chapter 11** at **11.4.2**.)

8.4 SUPPORTING DOCUMENTS AND DISCLOSURE

The 2008 Scheme Guide (section 5, paragraph 2) suggests that the decision letter will tell you 'what evidence we considered in order to reach our original decision'. In fact, more frequently, oblique reference may be made to different witnesses or a few lines of a pro forma medical report may be cited. The CICA does not, as a matter of practice, automatically send out copies of the documents it has relied on. In practical terms, in order to make a reasoned decision with regard to the merits of a review, the applicant should seek full disclosure of the material upon which the initial decision of the claims officer was based. This should not pose any real difficulty. If there is an issue with potentially sensitive disclosure of police information then disclosure of the gist of the evidence against the applicant should be sought in line with *R v. CICA, ex parte Leatherland, Brammall & Kay* [2001] ACD 13. Once this material is to hand, a proper assessment can be made of what, if any, further evidence may be available to further the applicant's case and who should obtain it.

8.5 WHO DEALS WITH THE REVIEW?

Under paragraph 60 of the 1996 and 2001 Schemes, the review decision would be taken by a claims officer 'more senior than the one who made the original decision'. However, under paragraph 60 of the 2008 Scheme it will simply be a 'claims officer other than the one who made the original decision'. The rationale behind this change is not entirely clear. The CICA's leaflet 'Changes to the Criminal Injuries Compensation Scheme' states that this change was to enable claims to be processed more quickly, but there is some suspicion that it is due to a shortage of more experienced or senior claims officers. In some cases of more significant value, ex-Board and Panel members appear to have been 'contracted in' by the CICA to act as claims officers. Their status within the CICA is not entirely clear. It is also noteworthy that the CICA is not uniformly willing to provide the identity of the claims officers concerned which can be frustrating for applicants and their representatives and can hinder productive communication.

8.6 TIMING AND OUTCOME OF THE REVIEW

There are no formal time limits within which the review decision will be made. The CICA's leaflet says:

> If we don't need further information we aim to tell you our decision within six weeks of passing your application to a claims officer. If we need further information we aim to tell you our decision within six weeks of receiving that information. We will keep you up to date throughout.

Under the 1996 and 2001 Schemes review decisions could take several months and in some cases much longer to determine. However, the CICA does appear to be processing review decisions more expeditiously now once the relevant evidence is to hand.

8.6.1 Provisional indication of award

In some cases, especially claims with more complex medical issues and loss of earnings claims, there has been an increased tendency by the CICA to use 'indicative awards'. The CICA may produce a schedule with a proposed breakdown of an award in such cases. This can be a really useful and effective tool to fine-tune the arguments on potential areas of difference between the parties and identify any relevant gaps in the evidence. In our experience the applicant has been permitted at this stage to produce further evidence in relation to the issues raised at this juncture with a view to attempting to secure an appropriate and fair award. The applicant may have much to gain by cooperating with this approach. He or she will still have the right to appeal if the final award is unacceptable for some reason.

8.6.2 Right to appeal review decision

As set out above, the right to appeal a review decision remains. However, the provisions in respect of the procedural aspects of appeals have been substantially amended. They appear at paragraph 61 of the 2008 Scheme and are dealt with in **Chapter 11** in detail.

9 RECONSIDERATION AND RE-OPENING OF FINAL DECISIONS

9.1 INTRODUCTION

This chapter covers the provisions in the 2008 Scheme relating to the reconsideration of final decisions made by the CICA or the First-tier Tribunal before actual payment of the award by the CICA and the re-opening of cases on medical grounds. These topics were covered in detail in Chapter 19 of *Criminal Injuries Compensation Claims* (Law Society, 2005) and many of the provisions remain largely unchanged from the provisions in the 2001 Scheme. There are, however, a few significant changes and this chapter outlines the procedural position under the 2008 Scheme.

9.2 RECONSIDERATION OF DECISIONS BEFORE PAYMENT OF AWARD

It has long been a feature of the statutory and earlier non-statutory Criminal Injuries Compensation Schemes that a decision can be reconsidered at any time prior to de facto payment of an award where there has been a change in circumstances or where there is new evidence. This is consistent with the Scheme providing payment from public funds to blameless victims of violent crime. The provision was found at paragraph 53 of the 1996 and 2001 Schemes and remains unchanged at paragraph 53 of the 2008 Scheme (save for the updating of terminology to refer to the First-tier Tribunal).

Therefore, pursuant to paragraph 53 of the 2008 Scheme, a claims officer may reconsider a decision 'at any time before actual payment of a final award where there is new evidence or a change in circumstances'. Most commonly this would be a recent conviction of the victim, or occasionally further witness evidence or medical evidence which calls into question the basis on which the decision had been made. This provision may relate to an initial decision or a review decision of the CICA. There is nothing in the wording to preclude a revision upwards as well as downwards, though the few reported cases concern revisions downwards and this accords with the authors' own experience (see, for example, *R* v. *CICB, ex parte Thomas* [1995] PIQR P99).

Procedurally, the position remains unchanged in that if the CICA has already sent written notification of the decision to the applicant, then the applicant will be sent a written notice that the decision is to be reconsidered and then has 30 days to make representations in this regard. See paragraph 54 of the 2008 Scheme. If the applicant is unhappy with the revised decision then, as before, he or she can seek a review if it was an initial decision (paragraph 58) or appeal if it was a review decision (paragraph 61).

Should further evidence or a change in circumstances come to light after a decision made by the Tribunal but before payment has been made by the CICA then, as before, paragraph 55 of the 2008 Scheme provides that:

> Where a decision to make an award has been made by a claims officer in accordance with a direction by the First-tier Tribunal on determining an appeal under paragraph 64, but before the award has been paid the claims officer considers that there is new evidence or a change in circumstances which justifies reconsidering whether the award should be withheld or the amount of compensation reduced, the Authority will refer the case to the First-tier Tribunal for rehearing.

As is evident, this provision envisages only withholding or reducing an award. It has never previously been the policy of the CICA or the old Board to reclaim previously paid interim payments even if a downwards revision is made or a finding on eligibility revised although there is arguably a power to do so. However, as noted at 4.2.4 above, paragraph 3 of Appendix 4 to the 2008 Scheme Guide does rather suggest that this policy might change.

9.3 RE-OPENING OF CASES ON MEDICAL GROUNDS

The old Board had the power to re-open cases under the 1979 and 1990 non-statutory Schemes where there had been a 'serious change' in the applicant's medical condition which was attributable to the original injury. This avoided the necessity for provisional awards and the uncertainties associated with making allowances in a final award for marked deterioration or degeneration.

9.3.1 Time limit for application to re-open

Under the 1990 Scheme the time limit for such an application was three years. Under the 1996 and 2001 Schemes the time limit was shortened to two years and the wording of the rule was slightly amended to permit re-opening where:

> there has been such a material change in the victim's medical condition that injustice would occur if the original assessment of compensation were allowed to stand, or where the victim has since died in consequence of the injury (paragraph 56).

Paragraph 57 stated:

> A case will not be re-opened more than two years after the date of the final decision unless the claims officer is satisfied, on the basis of evidence presented in support of the application to re-open the case, that the renewed application can be considered without a need for further extensive enquiries.

The wording of the provisions in respect of re-opening is the same in the 2008 Scheme as in the 1996 and 2001 Schemes (other than updating the terminology to refer to the First-tier Tribunal). They still appear at paragraphs 56 and 57 of the 2008 Scheme.

9.3.2 Restrictions on re-opening

Practitioners should note that where the prospect of future deterioration has been accounted for in the original award then it will remain inappropriate to re-open the award (see *R* v. *CICB, ex parte Brown*, unreported 12 December 1987, DC but cited in the CICB's Annual Report 1989). Further, the Scheme which applied to the original award is that which will be applied on consideration of re-opening.

9.3.3 Guidance on re-opening

Some useful guidance on this provision and its implementation in terms of examples can be found in the CICAP's Annual Report 2000–01 at paragraphs 5.14–5.23. The Guide to the 2001 Scheme made it clear that re-opening after a final decision was rare and could only happen if the medical condition had:

> substantially deteriorated in a way which was not expected when we made the decision; and it would be unfair for our decision to stand

and went on to cite examples such as no longer being able to work, or qualifying for a higher tariff award. The guidance to the 2008 Scheme has been simplified and the 2008 Scheme Guide(section 4, paragraphs 11 and 12) reads as follows:

> 11 Once you have accepted a final award and received your payment, your case will not be re-opened except in rare circumstances. We will only re-open a case if there has been such a change in your medical condition that an injustice would occur if the case were not re-opened, or in cases where a person has since died as a result of their injuries.
>
> 12 We will not normally re-open a case unless it is within two years of the final decision. If you ask us to re-open on medical grounds a case that has been closed for more than two years, you will have to give us enough evidence to support the case for re-opening.

In reality this means the applicant must be able to produce (if the CICA no longer has it) the medical evidence which was relied upon in making the initial decision and further medical evidence which demonstrates the material change in the applicant's medical condition and deals with causation in the sense required by the Scheme, i.e. direct attributability.

9.3.4 Test to be applied on re-opening

The points made by the Court of Appeal in *R* v. *CICB, ex parte Williams* [2000] PIQR Q339 in relation to the test to be applied to re-opening remain pertinent though that concerned a claim under the 1990 Scheme which called for a 'serious' rather than a 'material' change. In particular, the three-stage test propounded is as follows: first, there should be a change in the applicant's medical condition; that is a matter for pure comparison between the condition of the applicant at the date of the original award and his or her condition at the date he or she is seeking reconsideration. Second, the change has to amount to a serious change; this is a matter for judgement on the facts of the particular case. Third, the change has to be directly attributable to the original crime. Direct attributability requires an unbroken line of causation, unbroken by a new or supervening event which of itself was so powerful or dominant as to render the initial operating cause wholly nugatory. It is a matter of fact and degree in every case. Once serious change is established, the question is whether injustice would occur if the original assessment were allowed to stand. In that case the Board had proceeded on the basis of a report which contained a misdiagnosis that played no part in the test to be applied. The case could be re-opened because the deterioration in the applicant's back condition was due to activities that would take place in the ordinary course of daily life. They were not supervening new causes but part of a chain which was unbroken.

Other examples of re-opened cases are detailed in Chapter 19 of *Criminal Injuries Compensation Claims* (Law Society, 2005).

9.3.5 Procedural issues

In cases where it is possible that there might be a future significant deterioration the CICA and the old Panel and now the First-tier Tribunal will be willing to mark the file 'Do Not Destroy' for storage purposes just in case the matter does need to be restored. The most obvious claims will be those where there is a small but not insignificant risk of the development of epilepsy or perhaps of amputation should future surgery prove unsuccessful.

Paragraph 60(2) the 2008 Scheme provides:

> Where, on review of a decision not to re-open a case under paragraphs 56-57, the reviewing claims officer decides to re-open the case, he or she will proceed to determine the application for compensation. If the applicant is dissatisfied with that determination, he or she may appeal under paragraph 61.

This is a new provision which clarifies that where an initial decision to refuse an application to re-open a case has been reviewed successfully, the reviewing claims officer may proceed to deal with the application for compensation. The applicant retains his or her right of appeal and so is in the same position as any other applicant under the Scheme.

By paragraph 62, the 2008 Scheme further provides:

> Where the appeal concerns a decision not to re-open a case under paragraphs 56-57, and the application for re-opening was made more than two years after the date of the final decision, the First-tier Tribunal must be satisfied that the renewed application can be considered without a need for further extensive enquiries by the Authority.

This mirrors the position whereby the first of the conditions for waiver of the two-year time limit is that it is practicable for the application to be considered (see comments at 7.3 above).

10 APPEALING AGAINST CICA DECISIONS

10.1 INTRODUCTION

This chapter covers the provisions in the 2008 Scheme relating to appealing against review decisions and other decisions made by the CICA. This topic was covered in detail in Chapters 17 and 18 of *Criminal Injuries Compensation Claims* (Law Society, 2005) and some of the material in Chapter 17 relating to the grounds for an appeal remains relevant under the 2008 Scheme. However there have been a number of significant procedural changes to the entire appeals process by virtue of the 2008 Scheme, which are covered in full in this chapter. The new procedural rules governing the preparation for and conduct of appeal hearings are considered in detail in **Chapter 11** of this book.

10.2 OVERVIEW OF NEW PROVISIONS GOVERNING APPEALS

Whilst the CICA still determines the applications for compensation made under the 2008 Scheme, if the application is refused or the applicant is unhappy with the award, any appeal must be made to the First-tier Tribunal (Criminal Injuries Compensation), which replaces the previous appellate body, the Criminal Injuries Compensation Appeals Panel (CICAP). This First-tier Tribunal is an independent panel, set up by the Tribunals, Courts and Enforcement Act 2007. The Tribunal will be composed of legally qualified judges, medically qualified members and lay members, and the usual composition of a Tribunal will be one Judge and two members, one of whom is medically qualified.

10.2.1 Right to an appeal

The right of an appeal from a review decision remains unaltered at paragraph 61 of the 2008 Scheme which provides:

> An applicant who is dissatisfied with a decision taken on a review under paragraph 60(1) or with a determination under paragraph 60(2) may appeal against the decision to the First-tier Tribunal in accordance with Tribunal Procedure Rules.

However, the procedural rules in respect of appeals have been completely re-written. Formerly the rules in relation to appeals were contained in the body of the Scheme. Save in so far as paragraph 61 of the 2008 Scheme describes the circumstances in which appeals may be made, the rules in relation to appeals are now no longer part of the Scheme itself but governed by totally separate Tribunal Procedure (First-tier Tribunal) (Social Entitlement Chamber) Rules 2008, SI 2008/2685 (the 'Tribunal Procedure Rules', see **Appendix 3**) which apply to all existing CICA claims, not only claims under the 2008 Scheme. The enabling Act for these rules is the Tribunals, Courts and Enforcement Act 2007. These rules only apply in relation to appeals to the Tribunal. Once the appeal has been dealt with – if there is an extant claim (because the appeal was for example in respect of waiver of a time limit or other equivalent procedural point) then the claim is remitted to the CICA and the 'Scheme rules' apply. This chapter deals with the framework of the rules as they apply to making an appeal. The rules are heavily procedural and there is some complexity in this regard.

10.3 MAKING AN APPEAL – THE RULES

Section 5 of the 2008 Scheme Guide deals with reviews and appeals. It provides the following link in order to obtain the Tribunal Procedure Rules: **www.cicap.gov.uk/RulesLegislation/rulesLegislation.htm** (or a paper copy can be obtained by writing to the Tribunal). The rules do not only apply to criminal injuries claims; they also apply to asylum support, child support and social security appeal cases and so need to be consulted with care. Some of the provisions only apply to criminal injury claims. The rules break down into four parts. Part 1 deals with definitions and introductory matters, Part 2 deals with general powers and provisions, Part 3 deals with proceedings before the Tribunal and contains three chapters which deal with what happens before the hearing, during the hearing and the decisions and their content. Part 4 deals with correcting, setting aside, reviewing and appealing Tribunal decisions and applies only in a limited way to criminal injuries claims and is considered in further detail below. In similar terms to the overriding objective found in the Civil Procedure Rules 1998, rule 2 states the overriding objective to be applied by the Tribunal. The Tribunal must seek to give effect to the overriding objective when it: (a) exercises any power under these rules; or (b) interprets any rule or practice direction (rule 2(3)).

10.3.1 The overriding objective

The title of rule 2 is: 'Overriding objective and parties' obligation to co-operate with the Tribunal'. It is consonant with the policy considerations of and approach underlying the Scheme that emphasis is placed on cooperation of the parties, but this now includes the CICA as well as the appellant. The substance of rule 2 is as follows:

> (1) The overriding objective of these Rules is to enable the Tribunal to deal with cases fairly and justly.

(2) Dealing with a case fairly and justly includes –

(a) dealing with the case in ways which are proportionate to the importance of the case, the complexity of the issues, the anticipated costs and the resources of the parties;
(b) avoiding unnecessary formality and seeking flexibility in the proceedings;
(c) ensuring, so far as practicable, that the parties are able to participate fully in the proceedings;
(d) using any special expertise of the Tribunal effectively; and
(e) avoiding delay, so far as compatible with proper consideration of the issues.

[...]
(4) Parties must –

(a) help the Tribunal to further the overriding objective; and
(b) co-operate with the Tribunal generally.

10.3.2 The steps to be taken by the appellant

When a review decision is sent to an applicant, a pro forma appeal form is also sent to the applicant should he or she wish to appeal. As the 2008 Scheme Guide explains, the appellant should fill in the form, including the reasons why he or she is appealing and 'any extra material' and send it to the Tribunal rather than the CICA so that it gets it within 90 days of the date of the review decision. Thereafter the Tribunal will explain its procedures when it receives the request for an appeal. The content of the appeal notice is now very heavily prescribed and this is dealt with in detail below.

10.4 DEADLINES FOR APPEALS

By rule 22(2) (Part 3, Chapter 1, Before the hearing):

> An appellant must start proceedings by sending or delivering a notice of appeal to the Tribunal so that it is received –
>
> [...]
>
> (b) in criminal injuries compensation cases, within 90 days after the date of the decision being challenged.

The date of the decision rather than the date of receipt of that decision is the trigger for the 90 days to start running. This is substantively the same rule as under the old regime.

10.4.1 Extending the time for an appeal

Rule 22(6) provides:

> If the appellant provides the notice of appeal to the Tribunal later than the time required by paragraph (2) or by an extension of time allowed under rule 5(3)(a) (power to extend time) –

(a) the notice of appeal must include a request for an extension of time and the reason why the notice of appeal was not provided in time; and
(b) unless the Tribunal extends time for the notice of appeal under rule 5(3)(a) (power to extend time) the Tribunal must not admit the notice of appeal.

Rule 5 comes under Part 2 of the rules which deals with general powers and provisions. In particular, rule 5 deals with the case management powers of the Tribunal. Rule 5(3)(a) provides:

(3) In particular and without restricting the general powers in paragraphs (1) and (2), the Tribunal may –

(a) extend or shorten the time for complying with any rule, practice direction or direction;

Other than by reference to the overriding objective, there is no overt guidance to the Tribunal as to the criterion to be applied in exercising its discretion in considering this matter. The discretion therefore appears to be unfettered which may be contrasted with the position vis-à-vis a decision as to whether a review application ought to be permitted out of time (as to which see **Chapter 8**). However, the guidance on the Tribunal's website (**www.cicap.gov.uk**) 'Extending the 90 day limit' says:

In exceptional circumstances there may be good reasons why you cannot send your Notice of Appeal within the 90 day time limit. We may consider an extension to the 90 day limit if:

- it is based on good reasons, and
- it would be fair and just to do so

Example: If you are waiting for further medical reports that you must see before deciding whether or not to make an appeal then we may consider granting an extension whilst you wait for the documents to come to you [...]

Please tell us clearly why you need more time and how much longer you think you will need [...]

If we have received your appeal after the 90 day time limit, we will consider your application for an extension of time. We aim to consider your request within 5 days of receiving it. In some circumstances, your request will be referred to a Tribunal Judge [or] Member for a decision. We aim to notify you of any such decision and the reason for it within 3 weeks of receiving your request.

We will only admit your appeal if an extension is granted.

10.5 CONTENT OF THE APPEAL NOTICE

Rule 22 is prescriptive of the content of the appeal notice. In reality, if the pro forma sent by the CICA with the review decision is used, it should be relatively straightforward to comply with. Care should be taken to comply with it because there are now strike out powers available to the Tribunal under rule 8 which are considered in detail below. Rule 22(3) provides:

(3) The notice of appeal must be in English or Welsh, must be signed by the appellant and must state –

(a) the name and address of the appellant;
(b) the name and address of the appellant's representative (if any);
(c) an address where documents for the appellant may be sent or delivered;
(d) the name and address of any respondent;
(e) details (including the full reference) of the decision being appealed; and
(f) the grounds on which the appellant relies.

This provision encourages more reasoned appeal notices. It is likely that the previous practice in some cases of simply saying 'insufficient to compensate' or words to the effect of 'unfair decision' (admittedly often by lay clients who have no legal assistance or training) will be deemed inadequate and could theoretically trigger a full or partial strike out under rule 8. It is important that the appeal form is signed by the appellant.

10.6 EVIDENCE IN SUPPORT OF THE APPEAL

Rule 22(4) provides:

> The appellant must provide with the notice of appeal –
>
> (a) a copy of any written record of the decision being challenged;
> (b) any statement of reasons for that decision that the appellant has or can reasonably obtain;
> (c) any documents in support of the appellant's case which have not been supplied to the respondent; and
> (d) any further information or documents required by an applicable practice direction.

Under the old regime, the CICA would receive and process the appeal application, prepare the bundle and then forward everything to the CICAP in readiness for a hearing. Now the appellant has to send everything to the Tribunal. This includes a copy of the review decision of the CICA and any statement of reasons for this. Pursuant to rule 22(4)(c) any documents in support of the appellant's case which have not been supplied thus far to the CICA ought also to be supplied with the notice of appeal. The obvious implication is that any further evidence on which the appellant relies should be sent in with the appeal notice. The practice hitherto had been to notify the Tribunal that further evidence would be forthcoming and if there was some dispute with the CICA over further evidence a directions hearing might be listed in a substantial claim. The authors' experience thus far of the implementation of the new rules is that so long as the appellant identifies what further evidence he or she may seek to rely on and the likely timescale for the production of this evidence, the Tribunal will admit the notice. This accords with the guidance published on the Tribunal's own website which states (under the heading 'How to appeal'):

> If you are still waiting to receive documents from someone else, please advise us of when you expect to be able to send them to us. Unless you need these documents to help you to decide whether or not to appeal, please do not wait until you have them to send in your appeal form.

10.6.1 Practice directions

The reference in rule 22(4) to:

> (d) any further information or documents required by an applicable practice direction,

relates to the practice directions issued by the previous Chairman of the CICAP and Principal Judge, Mr Roger Goodier, on 3 November 2008. Copies of these practice directions can be downloaded from the Tribunal's website at **www.cicap.gov.uk** under 'Rules and Legislation' and are at **Appendix 4** of this book. They should be consulted closely. The purpose and function of these is to standardise case preparation and disclosure. The most relevant practice directions at this juncture for the appellant to consider will be the following:

CI-1 Claims for financial loss

This contains detailed requirements for disclosure in respect of loss of earnings and other financial loss claims. It is worded almost identically to the previous practice statement with regard to financial loss. However, it is worthy of note that paragraph 8 of this updated practice guidance provides:

> An Appellant who fails to comply with this direction risks having the claim for financial loss struck out either in full or in part, and/or having an award withheld or reduced under paragraph 13(c) of the Scheme for failing to give reasonable assistance in connection with the application.

CI-3 Specialist evidence

This practice statement requires joint instruction of experts where both parties agree that a specialist report is necessary, with the reasonable fee of the expert being paid by the CICA. Where there is disagreement about this between the parties, then an application ought to be made to the Tribunal in writing (by both parties) for directions. Paragraph 4 of this practice statement provides:

> Failure by or on behalf of the Appellant promptly or at all to disclose to the Authority and the Tribunal any specialist report in the possession of the Appellant relating directly or indirectly to the relevant injury may result in the Tribunal not admitting such evidence and/or striking out a part or the whole of a claim or deciding to withhold or reduce an award under paragraph 13(c) of the Scheme (failure to give reasonable assistance in connection with the application).

This guidance is consistent with the (in our opinion) rather poorly worded undertaking in the application form to disclose all relevant medical evidence to CICA. The policy behind it is easy to understand. The CICA and the Tribunal are dealing here with taxpayers' money and the process is inquisitorial rather than adversarial. Therefore arguably full disclosure ought to be provided if the appellant wants a share in the bounty provided by the taxpayer. In reality, however, the position is not so straightforward. Some victims' representatives remain of the view that medico-legal reports obtained by the appellant should remain privileged until and unless he or she wishes to disclose them (see *Carlson* v. *Townsend* [2001] EWCA Civ 511). That said, it is fair to observe that a tactical view will need to be taken when representing appellants in such circumstances. If the Tribunal considers that the appellant has not been totally forthright it has a broad discretion to reduce an award or deny one altogether on grounds of failure to cooperate. It may be better to disclose the negative report along with the other positive evidence and argue the claim on the merits.

10.7 PROCESSING THE APPEAL

By virtue of rule 22(7):

> The Tribunal must send a copy of the notice of appeal and any accompanying documents to each other party –
>
> [...]
>
> (b) in criminal injuries compensation cases, as soon as reasonably practicable after the Tribunal receives the notice of appeal.

There is no fixed timescale for the Tribunal to send the notice of appeal to the CICA. Once this step has been taken the CICA must then, pursuant to rule 24, send a response bundle to the Tribunal and to the appellant. There is no strict deadline for this step to be taken. The Tribunal's website comments that the CICA aims to do this within six weeks of receiving the notice of appeal, though in practice it may take longer. The content of the response is also prescribed, in this case by rule 24 which provides as follows:

> (1) When a decision maker receives the notice of appeal or a copy of it, the decision maker must send or deliver a response to the Tribunal –
>
> [...]
> (b) in other cases, as soon as reasonably practicable after the decision maker received the notice of appeal.
>
> (2) The response must state –
>
> (a) the name and address of the decision maker;
> (b) the name and address of the decision maker's representative (if any);
> (c) an address where documents for the decision maker may be sent or delivered;
> (d) the names and addresses of any other respondents and their representatives (if any);
> (e) whether the decision maker opposes the appellant's case and, if so, any grounds for such opposition which are not set out in any documents which are before the Tribunal; and
> (f) any further information or documents required by a practice direction or direction.
>
> (3) The response may include a submission as to whether it would be appropriate for the case to be disposed of without a hearing.
> (4) The decision maker must provide with the response –
>
> (a) a copy of any written record of the decision under challenge, and any statement of reasons for that decision, if they were not sent with the notice of appeal;

- (b) copies of all documents relevant to the case in the decision maker's possession, unless a practice direction or direction states otherwise; and
- (c) in cases to which rule 23 (cases in which the notice of appeal is to be sent to the decision maker) applies, a copy of the notice of appeal, any documents provided by the appellant with the notice of appeal and (if they have not otherwise been provided to the Tribunal) the name and address of the appellant's representative (if any).

(5) The decision maker must provide a copy of the response and any accompanying documents to each other party at the same time as it provides the response to the Tribunal.

(6) The appellant and any other respondent may make a written submission and supply further documents in reply to the decision maker's response.

(7) Any submission or further documents under paragraph (6) must be provided to the Tribunal within 1 month after the date on which the decision maker sent the response to the party providing the reply, and the Tribunal must send a copy to each other party.

In reality the responses from the CICA tend not to contain a reasoned justification for the review decision but a rather terse statement to the effect that it will stand by the review decision previously made. Along with the response, the CICA must provide a copy of its own previous decision (notwithstanding the fact that the appellant should already have sent this to the Tribunal) and copies of all documents relevant to the case in the decision maker's possession (unless a practice direction states otherwise). We are not aware of any such practice direction as at December 2009. In practice the CICA, in line with its previous practice, will also send a summary. This generally, according to the guidance on the Tribunal's website, will consist of the following:

- brief details of the incident
- details of your injuries
- the decisions made by the Authority
- the names of witnesses the Tribunal will invite to your hearing (if granted), and
- the issues raised by the Authority – these could relate to your eligibility to receive an award, or the amount of compensation you should receive. To find out more about eligibility, please refer to the 'Eligibility for an award' section of this website.

The appellant is well advised to study carefully the content of the summary. It does not fetter the investigation or inquiry into matters by the Tribunal but it will certainly be the starting point for the Tribunal's consideration of the appeal. It should be noted that pursuant to rule 24(3) the response may include a submission as to whether it would be appropriate for the case to be disposed of without a hearing. Normally the Tribunal will inform the appellant when it receives the CICA's response bundle whether the appeal will go to a hearing or be dealt with on paper. This issue is considered separately below. Once the CICA has replied then the appellant has one month from this date to provide any further arguments or documents which should be send direct to the appellant. This may properly consist of further evidence or skeleton arguments or the like. The Tribunal's website guidance states:

> The Tribunal may decide not to take into account documents that have not been supplied promptly. In some circumstances, there may be good reasons why you

cannot supply further documents within 1 month. If you need more time you can write to us to request an extension. Tell us why you need more time and how much longer you need. Your application will be considered by a Tribunal Judge or Member.

10.8 APPEALS IN RESPECT OF TIME LIMITS, RE-OPENING AND WITHDRAWAL OF AWARDS

Under the 1996 and 2001 Schemes the appeals in respect of what may be described as procedural matters (such as waiver of time limits) triggered a paper review by the Chairman or an adjudicator nominated by the Chairman pursuant to the rules at paragraphs 66–68 of those Schemes. A decision by the adjudicator or Chairman would be final. Those rules have been abolished and the new Tribunal Procedure Rules now govern these matters. If the appeal is in respect of a decision:

- not to waive or extend the time limit in paragraph 18 (application for compensation) or paragraph 59 (application for review) (58(1)(a)); or
- not to re-open a case under paragraphs 56–57 (58(1)(b)); or
- to withdraw an award under paragraph 50(1) (58(1)(f));

then the Tribunal Procedure Rules suggest that the Tribunal has a discretion to deal with the matter on paper without a hearing and that if a decision is made on paper no appeal will lie. Therefore, partially replicating the position under the older Schemes, rule 27 in Chapter 2 of the Tribunal Procedure Rules deals with decisions with or without hearings. This rule provides:

> (1) Subject to the following paragraphs, the Tribunal must hold a hearing before making a decision which disposes of proceedings unless –
>
> (a) each party has consented to, or has not objected to, the matter being decided without a hearing; and
> (b) the Tribunal considers that it is able to decide the matter without a hearing.
>
> (2) This rule does not apply to decisions under Part 4.
> (3) The Tribunal may in any event dispose of proceedings without a hearing under rule 8 (striking out a party's case).
> (4) In a criminal injuries compensation case –
>
> (a) the Tribunal may make a decision which disposes of proceedings without a hearing; and
> (b) subject to paragraph (5), if the Tribunal makes a decision which disposes of proceedings without a hearing, any party may make a written application to the Tribunal for the decision to be reconsidered at a hearing.
>
> (5) An application under paragraph (4)(b) may not be made in relation to a decision –
>
> (a) not to extend a time limit;
> (b) not to set aside a previous decision;
> (c) not to allow an appeal against a decision not to extend a time limit; or
> (d) not to allow an appeal against a decision not to reopen a case.

(6) An application under paragraph (4)(b) must be received within 1 month after the date on which the Tribunal sent notice of the decision to the party making the application.

The discretion to deal with the matter without a hearing is at rule 27(1)(b). The rules do not prescribe that the decision must be made without a hearing, nor do they give any indication of how the discretion could or should be exercised. It is interesting to note that the CICA's leaflet entitled 'Appealing against a Review Decision' which can be found on its website says that:

If you are appealing because:

- we refused to consider your case because of a time limit; or
- you asked us to open your case again because your medical condition had changed, but we refused to do so;

a Tribunal Member or Tribunal Judge will decide your appeal on the papers. Their decision is final.

It seems likely, therefore, that the reality is that (unless challenged by the appellant), as under the old regime, such appeals will be dealt with on paper and the decision will be final notwithstanding the residual discretion contained in the rules.

10.8.1 Successful procedural appeals

If the appeal is allowed then the position is very similar to the outcome under the old regime in that the Tribunal will direct the CICA to deal with the matter as if the appeal had not been required (see paragraph 63(1) of the 2008 Scheme). The Tribunal will effectively remit the matter to the CICA for consideration of the claim. The claim goes back to the stage it would have been at but for the refusal or decision by the CICA which is appealed against. Hence, for example, paragraph 63 continues:

(2) In a case where the appeal was against a decision not to waive the time limit in paragraph 18, the First-tier Tribunal will direct the Authority to arrange for the application for compensation to be dealt with under this Scheme as if the time limit had been waived by a claims officer.

This relates to a claim where a waiver of the usual two-year limit for all claims has been obtained successfully on appeal before the Tribunal. The claim is effectively remitted by the Tribunal to the CICA and is treated as a 'new' claim and may be subject to review or appeal as any other claim would.

See further, in paragraph 63, another example:

(3) In a case where the appeal was against a decision not to extend the time limit in paragraph 59, the First-tier Tribunal will direct the Authority to conduct a review under paragraph 60.

This relates to an appeal where the CICA had refused to waive the 90-day time limit in respect of an application for a review decision but the Tribunal has allowed the appeal. Again, the claim is effectively remitted by the Tribunal to the CICA for the review decision to be taken by it. The applicant will retain his or her right to appeal the review decision under paragraph 61.

10.9 APPEALS IN RESPECT OF AWARDS

Under the 1996 and 2001 Schemes a member of the Panel's staff could refer the case for an oral hearing under paragraphs 72–78 of those Schemes where the decision was in respect of an award. The discretion was fairly broad but he or she would be bound to refer an application to an oral hearing if the question was whether the injury was sufficiently serious to qualify for the minimum award or where there was a dispute as to the material facts or conclusions upon which a review decision was based (paragraph 70, 1996 and 2001 Schemes). Under the 2008 Scheme a decision:

- withholding an award (including a decision to withhold on reconsideration of an award);
- making an award, including a decision to make a reduced award;
- requiring repayment of an award (this is in circumstances where under paragraphs 48 and 49 the CICA may seek repayment because the applicant has received other compensation or even UK social security benefits – see further **Chapter 5** at **5.3** in this regard);

will generally lead to an oral hearing. Rule 27(1) of the Tribunal Rules provides:

> the Tribunal must hold a hearing before making a decision which disposes of proceedings unless –
>
> (a) each party has consented to, or has not objected to, the matter being decided without a hearing; and
> (b) the Tribunal considers that it is able to decide the matter without a hearing.

The basic rule is, therefore, similar to the old regime in that one proceeds to a hearing unless an agreement has been reached by all the parties to deal with it on paper and the matter is one which the Tribunal considers it can decide without a hearing. (This rule is broadly equivalent to the paragraph 78 provision under the 1996 and 2001 Schemes.) As above, there is no guidance within the rules as to any discretion on the part of the Tribunal in determining whether it is able to decide the matter without a hearing. If the appeal is dealt with without a hearing and the appellant is unhappy with the outcome, then the applicant retains a right of appeal under rule 27(4)(b):

> any party may make a written application to the Tribunal for the decision to be reconsidered at a hearing.

Paragraph 27(6) provides that:

> An application under paragraph (4)(b) must be received within 1 month after the date on which the Tribunal sent notice of the decision to the party making the application.

10.9.1 Successful appeals in respect of awards:

Under paragraph 64 of the 2008 Scheme:

> Where the First-tier Tribunal allows an appeal against a decision taken on review under paragraph 58(1)(c), (d) or (e) it will make such direction as it thinks appropriate as to the decision to be made by a claims officer on the application for

compensation, but any such direction must be in accordance with the relevant provisions of this Scheme.

Under paragraph 65 when making a decision in respect of any of these matters the Tribunal may:

(a) on an application or adjournment [...] direct that an interim payment be made; and
(b) where an appeal is found to be frivolous or vexatious the First-tier Tribunal may reduce the amount of compensation to be awarded by such amount as it considers appropriate.

The discretion here is unfettered and there is no real guidance on how it would be exercised. The Tribunal will consider whether a conclusion as to the level of award and any special expenses may be determined at that juncture or whether further evidence is required and if so give directions in that regard.

The procedural rules relevant to the preparation for and conduct of appeal hearings are considered in detail in **Chapter 11**.

11 PROCEDURAL RULES FOR APPEAL HEARINGS

11.1 INTRODUCTION

There have been a number of significant procedural changes to the appeals process under the 2008 Scheme which are outlined in detail in **Chapter 10** of this book. The most significant change is that any appeal against a decision made by the CICA must be made to the First-tier Tribunal (Criminal Injuries Compensation), (referred to in this book as the 'First-tier Tribunal' or 'Tribunal'), which replaces the previous appellate body, the Criminal Injuries Compensation Appeals Panel (CICAP). This First-tier Tribunal is an independent panel, set up by the Tribunals, Courts and Enforcement Act 2007. This chapter outlines the new procedural rules governing the preparation for, and conduct of, appeal hearings.

11.2 RULES FOR PREPARATION AND CONDUCT OF HEARINGS

The general rules which form the framework for the appeal procedure have been outlined in **Chapter 10**. Prior to the introduction of these rules there was little in the way of formalities in terms of the method of service or other procedural matters. Furthermore, there were no real sanctions for failure to comply with directions save ultimately the threat on the horizon in more extreme cases of a reduction for an overall failure to cooperate. So, whilst it is fair to observe that the Tribunal and its predecessors have long regulated their own practice and procedure, the new rules are much more comprehensive and bring the procedural aspects of the appeals process much more closely in alignment with civil proceedings. Whether this is conducive to a regime which can be navigated effectively by a layman must be open to question.

11.2.1 The Tribunal Procedure Rules

As outlined in **Chapter 10**, the new rules are called the Tribunal Procedure (First-tier Tribunal) (Social Entitlement Chamber) Rules 2008, SI 2008/2685 (the 'Tribunal Procedure Rules': see **Appendix 3**) and the enabling Act for these Rules is the Tribunals, Courts and Enforcement Act 2007. Relevant extracts from the new

Tribunal Procedure Rules are also set out in this chapter and **Chapter 10**. The Tribunal Procedure Rules do not only apply to criminal injuries claims; they also apply to asylum support, child support and social security appeal cases and so need to be consulted with care. Some of the provisions only apply to criminal injury claims. It is probably most convenient to consider the rules by reference to the subdivisions between the different parts as set out below:

- Part 1: Definitions and introductory matters.
- Part 2: General powers and provisions.
- Part 3: Proceedings before the Tribunal.
- Part 4: Correcting, setting aside, reviewing and appealing Tribunal decisions.

11.3 PART 1: DEFINITIONS AND INTRODUCTORY MATTERS

The overriding objective contained in rule 2 has been considered in detail in **Chapter 10** at **10.3.1**. Otherwise this Part contains an explanation of the basic definitions to be applied in terms of the parties and terms used in the rules which may not be so obvious to a layman.

11.4 PART 2: GENERAL POWERS AND PROVISIONS

The general power to extend a time limit by virtue of rule 5(3) has been covered in **Chapter 10** of this book at **10.4.1**, but the whole of rule 5 is worthy of repetition:

(1) Subject to the provisions of the 2007 Act and any other enactment, the Tribunal may regulate its own procedure.
(2) The Tribunal may give a direction in relation to the conduct or disposal of proceedings at any time, including a direction amending, suspending or setting aside an earlier direction.
(3) In particular, and without restricting the general powers in paragraphs (1) and (2), the Tribunal may –

(a) extend or shorten the time for complying with any rule, practice direction or direction;
(b) consolidate or hear together two or more sets of proceedings or parts of proceedings raising common issues, or treat a case as a lead case (whether in accordance with rule 18 (lead cases) or otherwise);
(c) permit or require a party to amend a document;
(d) permit or require a party or another person to provide documents, information, evidence or submissions to the Tribunal or a party;
(e) deal with an issue in the proceedings as a preliminary issue;
(f) hold a hearing to consider any matter, including a case management issue;
(g) decide the form of any hearing;
(h) adjourn or postpone a hearing;
(i) require a party to produce a bundle for a hearing;
(j) stay (or, in Scotland, sist) proceedings;
(k) transfer proceedings to another court or tribunal if that other court or tribunal has jurisdiction in relation to the proceedings and –

(i) because of a change of circumstances since the proceedings were started, the Tribunal no longer has jurisdiction in relation to the proceedings; or

(ii) the Tribunal considers that the other court or tribunal is a more appropriate forum for the determination of the case; or

(l) suspend the effect of its own decision pending the determination by the Tribunal or the Upper Tribunal of an application for permission to appeal against, and any appeal or review of, that decision.

These powers do not at first blush hold any great surprises and (k) and (l) are highly unlikely to be relevant to CICA claims. As noted above the Tribunal has long been able to regulate its own procedure, to adjourn at will or make directions or revise directions previously made.

11.4.1 Power to compel witnesses

Rule 5(3)(d) enables the Tribunal to permit or require a party or another person to provide documents, information, evidence or submissions to the Tribunal or a party. It has long been the case that the police and witnesses might be requested to provide evidence or attend hearings. However, there were no 'teeth' to compel attendance or disclosure of records. The CICA or Tribunal was dependent upon the goodwill of the individual or organisation. The new regime is different because the stated power now does have teeth by way of the power to summons witnesses pursuant to rule 16 which provides:

(1) On the application of a party or on its own initiative, the Tribunal may –

(a) by summons (or, in Scotland, citation) require any person to attend as a witness at a hearing at the time and place specified in the summons or citation; or

(b) order any person to answer any questions or produce any documents in that person's possession or control which relate to any issue in the proceedings.

(2) A summons or citation under paragraph (1)(a) must –

(a) give the person required to attend 14 days' notice of the hearing or such shorter period as the Tribunal may direct; and

(b) where the person is not a party, make provision for the person's necessary expenses of attendance to be paid, and state who is to pay them.

(3) No person may be compelled to give any evidence or produce any document that the person could not be compelled to give or produce on a trial of an action in a court of law in the part of the United Kingdom where the proceedings are due to be determined.

(4) A summons, citation or order under this rule must –

(a) state that the person on whom the requirement is imposed may apply to the Tribunal to vary or set aside the summons, citation or order, if they have not had an opportunity to object to it; and

(b) state the consequences of failure to comply with the summons, citation or order.

The rule recognises that there may be some cases where public interest immunity arguments might be raised and appropriate objections might be aired before the

Tribunal. However, this puts the onus back on to the police, local authority, employer or whoever may be on the receiving end of the witness summons to raise such objections to the Tribunal giving the appellant, and presumably the CICA, an opportunity to make representations. This power is a welcome addition to the armoury of the Tribunal. The authors have not yet seen this used in practice and it remains to be seen how often and in what circumstances it will be deployed. There is concern in some quarters that appellants might abuse this power and make multiple applications for summonses against public bodies for documents which may only have marginal relevance to the issues to be determined. It is likely in the authors' view that the Tribunal will be cautious in such circumstances to ensure that the summons is appropriately tightly worded.

11.4.2 Directions hearings

Pursuant to rule 5(3)(f) a hearing may be held to consider any issue including a case management issue. This is the formal provision by which directions hearings may be held by the Tribunal. Directions hearings do now appear to have become much more commonplace. The authors have encountered hearings where it is apparent that there has been a discussion of the matters in issue between the Presenting Officer (for the CICA) and the Tribunal prior to the commencement of the hearing. While this may be thought to be efficacious, we think it is safer for all such discussions to take place in the appellant's presence so as to preserve the appearance and reality of fairness. In more complex cases, where there are genuine issues with regard to the need for different types of expert evidence, it is probably desirable and proportionate to have a directions hearing and it accords with the practice statement CI-3 issued by the former Principal Judge. One practical difficulty which has arisen in the authors' experience is that many Tribunals seek the directions to be by way of a live hearing with attendance by the appellant and his or her representatives if there are any. In some cases this can mean that an appellant (who will almost always be funding his or her claim out of the damages he or she may ultimately receive) will be paying for the cost of a lawyer to attend. In many cases this approach is not necessary or desirable and consideration should actively be given to whether the directions hearing can be disposed of appropriately by way of a telephone hearing (rule 5(3)(g) allows the Tribunal to decide the form of the hearing). Indeed, in other cases there may not need to be a hearing at all and directions could be made on paper it seems: see further in this regard rule 6 which provides:

> (1) The Tribunal may give a direction on the application of one or more of the parties or on its own initiative.
> (2) An application for a direction may be made –
>
> (a) by sending or delivering a written application to the Tribunal; or
> (b) orally during the course of a hearing.
>
> (3) An application for a direction must include the reason for making that application.
> (4) Unless the Tribunal considers that there is good reason not to do so, the

Tribunal must send written notice of any direction to every party and to any other person affected by the direction.

(5) If a party or any other person sent notice of the direction under paragraph (4) wishes to challenge a direction which the Tribunal has given, they may do so by applying for another direction which amends, suspends or sets aside the first direction.

It is also worthy of note that rule 6(5) suggests that any party affected by a direction may apply for another direction which amends, suspends or sets aside the first direction. It is not clear whether a differently constituted Tribunal will hear or consider the application at a hearing or on paper which may amount effectively to an appeal against an earlier directions order. Such an approach would appear to be in the interests of justice. Rule 15 provides further guidance with regard to the content of directions which may be given in relation to evidence and submissions. This rule supplements the general case management powers available to the Tribunal and provides that:

(1) [. . .] the Tribunal may give directions as to –

(a) issues on which it requires evidence or submissions;
(b) the nature of the evidence or submissions it requires;
(c) whether the parties are permitted or required to provide expert evidence;
(d) any limit on the number of witnesses whose evidence a party may put forward, whether in relation to a particular issue or generally;
(e) the manner in which any evidence or submissions are to be provided, which may include a direction for them to be given –
    (i) orally at a hearing; or
    (ii) by written submissions or witness statement; and
(f) the time at which any evidence or submissions are to be provided.

The Tribunal and its predecessors have always had the ability to regulate their approach to evidence and procedure and had a wide discretion in terms of the admissibility of evidence including hearsay evidence. That general power and discretion remains.

11.4.3 Nature of directions

Since the introduction of the new Tribunal Procedure Rules, there has been a tendency in some appeals for directions to be approached by Tribunal members along more adversarial lines than has previously been the case. For example, asking for a schedule to be produced initially by the appellant and a counter-schedule from the CICA. Alternatively, where two experts have previously been instructed, directing that questions be put to both, even if the earlier expert has not examined the appellant for a considerable period of time, and where that expert's evidence (obtained at first instance by the CICA) may be viewed as having been superseded by a later instructed expert. This practice does not appear to be consistent with the application of the policy underlying the Scheme generally and the guidance given by the Court of Appeal in *C (A Child)* v. *Secretary of State for the Home Department* [2004] EWCA Civ 234 (discussed in detail in Chapter 14 of *Criminal Injuries Compensation Claims* (Law Society, 2005)). Most appellants fund the management and running of their claims out of their damages by way of contingency fee arrangements or deferred costs arrangements. The lawyers who take on these claims need to be astute to minimise the legal costs associated with their management of these claims. It is fair to say that much of the time the directions proposed are sensible and proportionate and enable the lawyer to balance those requirements against proper case management. However, Tribunal members should be alive to the fact that a more adversarial approach to directions may impose additional legal costs on represented victims which will only serve to diminish the damages they may receive and will complicate matters for those who are unrepresented. Such an approach is also not consistent with the inquisitorial nature of the proceedings.

11.5 ADJOURNMENT OR POSTPONEMENT OF HEARINGS

The Tribunal and its predecessors have always regulated their proceedings in their own way, adjourning or postponing a hearing if they considered it appropriate. However, it has historically been very rare for the Tribunal to agree to a postponement or adjournment in advance of the date listed and generally an attendance has been required (with the expense this incurs). Practice statement CI-5 'Listing of appeal hearings; postponement of hearings' should be consulted where an appellant wishes to postpone a hearing in advance of the date listed or without an attendance. (See **Appendix 4** in this regard.) Understandably, the concern of the Tribunal is the potential wasting of resources and delay. 'Postponement' relates to taking the matter out of the list before the hearing and 'adjournment' relates to the position where after the hearing has commenced the Tribunal decides to put off making a final decision. Once the Tribunal has confirmed there should be an oral hearing then the parties have an obligation to provide in writing and with reasons any dates to avoid (paragraph 3). It is made plain that only in exceptional circumstances will non-availability due to work commitments or unavailability of a particular representative be a valid reason to postpone a hearing. (Anecdotal experience suggests that generally note will be taken of counsel's/solicitor's dates to avoid when the initial listing takes place but trying to shift the hearing date thereafter is difficult.) The Tribunal's policy with regard to listing appears in the body of this practice statement. Generally the Tribunal will give at least 14 days' notice of the hearing (often it is considerably longer) and, pursuant to paragraph 8, once notice of the hearing has been given, the presumption will be that the Tribunal will refuse a postponement request. Only where there are compellingly good reasons for the late postponement request will the hearing be postponed in advance of the hearing date. For these reasons it is crucially important that once notification is received by the Tribunal to the effect that an oral hearing is to be held the appellant should review the evidence and check that he or she really is ready to proceed to a hearing. If there are loose ends in terms of further questions to doctors which may take time to sort out, or further witness evidence is awaited, then the appellant must take the initiative and apply for further directions rather than automatically providing dates to avoid. If an application for postponement does need to be made, then it must be made in writing supported by evidence (e.g. a medical certificate). The original listing will stand – even if both the appellant and

Authority agree to a postponement, until and unless they are notified otherwise by the Tribunal. In the authors' view, even if the CICA withdraws its opposition to the appeal, the Tribunal remains seized of the matter. In our opinion, therefore, the absence of written confirmation from the Tribunal to the effect that it agrees the appeal, the appellant should still attend. An application may also be made on the day of the hearing and will be considered having regard to the policy of the Tribunal.

11.5.1 Listing of eligibility issues

Further in this connection, practice statement CI-2 'Listing of Appeal Hearings – Eligibility issues'(see **Appendix 4**) provides that following the CICA's response to the notice of appeal, if the Tribunal is satisfied that there should be an oral hearing, the appeal will be listed for hearing on the first available date after one month from the date of the CICA's response. Paragraph 2 of this practice statement provides:

> At the hearing, the tribunal may refuse to admit an eligibility issue not previously raised by the Authority unless good cause is shown for the delay in raising it or there is new evidence or a change in circumstances.

This is a welcome provision, especially if the CICA has been haphazard in its approach to the claim and the gathering of evidence and has chopped and changed its position or its requirements of the appellant. The general practice previously adopted was that if the CICA took the appellant 'by surprise' at the hearing and pursued issues which had not previously been raised, an adjournment might be considered. It now permits the Tribunal to press on, putting any new issues to one side if this is considered appropriate. Paragraph 3 of the practice statement provides:

> At the hearing on eligibility, if the Tribunal decides that the Appellant is eligible to an award of compensation, it will proceed to assess compensation at that hearing only if there is sufficient evidence fairly so to do – if not, it will adjourn and give directions.

This is useful confirmation for appellants who have been rejected as ineligible at the review stage. It means that they need not be overly concerned about their medical evidence and evidence in support of special expenses until and unless they get a finding in their favour (so long as some medical evidence confirms at least a level 1 injury directly attributable to the alleged crime of violence).

11.6 PREPARATION OF BUNDLES

Hitherto, the bundles have been prepared by the CICA. The position now is that the CICA sends a paginated bundle of all the documents it has had to the Tribunal. Thereafter any additional documents (e.g. those provided by the appellant such as schedules and skeleton arguments) are added to this bundle as 'T' labelled documents added to the end of the bundle. Plainly it is appropriate that this burden does not fall to the appellant. However, practitioners should scrutinise the bundle when received in advance of the hearing and ensure that any missing documents are brought to the attention of the Tribunal and inserted in advance of the hearing (preferably by two weeks before the hearing because the bundles are forwarded to Tribunal members generally 7–14 days prior to the sitting).

11.7 FAILURE TO COMPLY WITH RULES

Rule 7 deals with the consequences of failure to comply with rules. It is plain from rule 7(1) that:

> An irregularity resulting from a failure to comply with any requirement in these Rules, a practice direction or a direction, does not of itself render void the proceedings or any step taken in the proceedings.

That said, rule 7 provides certain other powers for the Tribunal:

> (2) If a party has failed to comply with a requirement in these Rules, a practice direction or a direction, the Tribunal may take such action as it considers just, which may include –
>
> (a) waiving the requirement;
> (b) requiring the failure to be remedied;
> (c) exercising its power under rule 8 (striking out a party's case); or
> (d) exercising its power under paragraph (3).
>
> (3) The Tribunal may refer to the Upper Tribunal, and ask the Upper Tribunal to exercise its power under section 25 of the 2007 Act in relation to, any failure by a person to comply with a requirement imposed by the Tribunal –
>
> (a) to attend at any place for the purpose of giving evidence;
> (b) otherwise to make themselves available to give evidence;
> (c) to swear an oath in connection with the giving of evidence;
> (d) to give evidence as a witness;
> (e) to produce a document; or
> (f) to facilitate the inspection of a document or any other thing (including any premises).

In reality the Tribunal will not exercise its power under rule 7(3). It is plain from the regime as it applies to criminal injuries claims that recourse may only be had beyond the First-tier Tribunal to the Upper Tier Tribunal, i.e. effectively the administrative court, in circumstances akin to those where judicial review could properly be considered.

11.7.1 Strike out provisions

One possible sanction for failure to abide by the rules or practice directions is to exercise the power to strike out a party's case pursuant to rule 8. This is a strike out without a hearing. Care needs to be taken by practitioners especially where the practice directions or any directions given by the Tribunal have threatened this sanction. Failure to abide by the order or direction will lead to an automatic strike out. Rule 8 provides as follows:

> (1) The proceedings, or the appropriate part of them, will automatically be struck out if the appellant has failed to comply with a direction that stated that failure

by a party to comply with the direction would lead to the striking out of the proceedings or that part of them.

(2) The Tribunal must strike out the whole or a part of the proceedings if the Tribunal –

(a) does not have jurisdiction in relation to the proceedings or that part of them; and
(b) does not exercise its power under rule 5(3)(k)(i) (transfer to another court or tribunal) in relation to the proceedings or that part of them.

(3) The Tribunal may strike out the whole or a part of the proceedings if –

(a) the appellant has failed to comply with a direction which stated that failure by the appellant to comply with the direction could lead to the striking out of the proceedings or part of them;
(b) the appellant has failed to co-operate with the Tribunal to such an extent that the Tribunal cannot deal with the proceedings fairly and justly; or
(c) the Tribunal considers there is no reasonable prospect of the appellant's case, or part of it, succeeding.

(4) The Tribunal may not strike out the whole or a part of the proceedings under paragraph (2) or (3)(b) or (c) without first giving the appellant an opportunity to make representations in relation to the proposed striking out.
(5) If the proceedings, or part of them, have been struck out under paragraph (1) or (3)(a), the appellant may apply for the proceedings, or part of them, to be reinstated.
(6) An application under paragraph (5) must be made in writing and received by the Tribunal within 1 month after the date on which the Tribunal sent notification of the striking out to the appellant.

Where (i) the strike out relates to an issue over whether the Tribunal has jurisdiction in relation to the proceedings; or (ii) the reason for the proposed strike out is failure to cooperate with the Tribunal; or (iii) the proposed strike out is because the claim has no reasonable prospects of success then the Tribunal must give the appellant notice of the proposed strike out. Once notice has been given, the appellant has one month from the date of the sending of the notification to make written representations as to why the strike out ought not to proceed. It appears that this will be determined not by way of an oral hearing, but rather on paper, though there is no express provision in the rules to this effect. The strike out regime applies equally to the CICA and the appellant save that rather than being struck out, the CICA or respondent is barred from taking further part in the proceedings. (See rule 8(7) below.) Therefore there may be situations where if for example the CICA was dragging its heels unnecessarily or it had changed tack substantially to the disadvantage of the appellant it could be barred from taking further part in the proceedings by the Tribunal. Rule 8 further provides as follows:

(7) This rule applies to a respondent as it applies to an appellant except that –

(a) a reference to the striking out of the proceedings is to be read as a reference to the barring of the respondent from taking further part in the proceedings; and
(b) a reference to an application for the reinstatement of proceedings which have been struck out is to be read as a reference to an application for the lifting of the bar on the respondent from taking further part in the proceedings.

(8) If a respondent has been barred from taking further part in proceedings under this rule and that bar has not been lifted, the Tribunal need not consider any response or other submission made by that respondent.

11.8 DECISIONS WITHOUT A HEARING

In relation to strike out, practitioners should also have regard to rule 27 (Part 3, Chapter 2 'Hearings') which gives the Tribunal the right to make a decision which disposes of proceedings without a hearing in the following terms:

(1) Subject to the following paragraphs, the Tribunal must hold a hearing before making a decision which disposes of proceedings unless –

(a) each party has consented to, or has not objected to, the matter being decided without a hearing; and
(b) the Tribunal considers that it is able to decide the matter without a hearing.

(2) This rule does not apply to decisions under Part 4.
(3) The Tribunal may in any event dispose of proceedings without a hearing under rule 8 (striking out a party's case).
(4) In a criminal injuries compensation case –

(a) the Tribunal may make a decision which disposes of proceedings without a hearing; and
(b) subject to paragraph (5), if the Tribunal makes a decision which disposes of proceedings without a hearing, any party may make a written application to the Tribunal for the decision to be reconsidered at a hearing.

(5) An application under paragraph (4)(b) may not be made in relation to a decision –

(a) not to extend a time limit;
(b) not to set aside a previous decision;
(c) not to allow an appeal against a decision not to extend a time limit; or
(d) not to allow an appeal against a decision not to reopen a case.

(6) An application under paragraph (4)(b) must be received within 1 month after the date on which the Tribunal sent notice of the decision to the party making the application.

Therefore where there has been no objection to the matter being dealt with without a hearing and the Tribunal thinks it can make a decision without a hearing then the Tribunal may proceed and may make a decision which disposes of the proceedings, e.g. a finding against the appellant on eligibility. The authors understand that the thinking behind this is that in hopeless claims or where there has been patchy cooperation from the appellant, the Tribunal may seize the initiative and deal with claims in a more pre-emptive manner and then this places the onus on the appellant to make a written application for reconsideration at a hearing (rule 27(4)(b)). It is anticipated that a fairly high proportion of cases will fall by the wayside at this juncture, especially if the appellants are not represented. It also removes the hurdle for the Tribunal of having to notify the appellant of its intention to strike out part or all of an appeal (rule 8(4)). It must, however, be questionable whether use of this provision, especially where victims are vulnerable and unrepresented, is consonant with the interests of justice.

11.9 COSTS AND EXPENSES

It has long been the position under the old Schemes that there was no power to award costs though a party may have legal representation. This situation continues and is confirmed by rule 10.

11.9.1 Cost of medical and other expert reports

Though there is no power to award legal costs, it remains the position that there may be circumstances in which a party may recover the cost of medical evidence provided to the Tribunal for the purpose of the appeal. If the parties follow the practice statement at CI-3 regarding specialist evidence then in theory it is unlikely that the CICA would not already have met the cost of the medical reports in accordance with its duty under paragraph 21 of the 2008 Scheme requiring an 'examination of the injury' and the Court of Appeal's guidance laid down by Sedley LJ in *C (A Child)* v. *Secretary of State for the Home Department* [2004] EWCA Civ 234. See also rule 20(2)(b) which provides that the Tribunal may meet reasonable expenses:

> incurred by the appellant in connection with any arrangements made by the Tribunal for the inspection of the appellant's injury.

However, in reality, especially in more complex claims and, in particular, some brain injury cases it may be that the appellant has privately funded further reports. The practice statement makes the point at paragraph 2:

> Save in exceptional circumstances, the Tribunal will not normally direct the Authority to reimburse to an Appellant any fee or part of a fee paid by or on behalf of the Appellant to a specialist where the Appellant has not given notice to the Authority of the intention to commission a report from a specialist and has not sought to agree with the Authority the need for the relevant report and the identity of the specialist to be instructed.

Therefore, should the appellant wish to stand any chance of recovering the costs of medical or nursing reports, they should give notice to the CICA and attempt to agree the expert. In the authors' experience if, as a matter of fact, the Tribunal has found the evidence helpful in the course of the appeal and some weight has been placed on it, so long as notice has been given, the Tribunal will be inclined towards directing payment by the CICA for the report(s). Frequently a contribution rather than the entire sum will be paid. Much will depend on the reasonableness of the fee. The appellant or his or her representative ought to come to the appeal hearing armed with the fee notes to be provided at the end of the hearing.

11.9.2 Witness expenses

It should be remembered that there is power to award the appellant and his or her witnesses' reasonable expenses in attending a hearing to give evidence. This does not include persons attending to give moral support only. This has long been the position but is now formally the case under rule 20. Appellants and their witnesses should request reimbursement from the clerks who manage the reception desk at the appeal hearing. Unfortunately the practice of providing immediate cash payments for travel costs under £20 has now gone and tickets need to be provided and a form filled in before reimbursement is provided at a later date. Should the appellant or witnesses not be able to travel by public transport and wish to claim the cost of a taxi, a note from their GP or treating doctor to that effect ought to be provided otherwise the cost of the taxi will not be met by the public purse.

11.10 REPRESENTATIVES

Rule 11 deals with representatives. It has always been the case that an appellant was entitled to be represented although there was no power to order the costs of representation to be paid, as remains the case. If a representative is appointed then the Tribunal should be informed in writing of their name and address and the Tribunal shall send this on to the CICA. By rule 11(5):

> Anything permitted or required to be done by a party under these Rules, a practice direction or a direction may be done by the representative of that party, except signing a witness statement.

Once a representative has been notified then all correspondence should be sent to the representative and it is assumed that the representative continues as authorised to act until or unless written notification is given otherwise. At the hearing of the appeal pursuant to rule 11(7) an appellant who has been unrepresented to date can attend with another person who:

> [...] with the permission of the Tribunal, may act as a representative or otherwise assist in presenting the party's case at the hearing.

Prior notice does not need to be provided of this person/representative. This allows a 'McKenzie friend' or other layman to attend and represent or assist the appellant. The Tribunal, and before it the Panel, had the same power and would in appropriate situations exclude an individual as a representative. (See in this regard *Re William Rennie Templeton*, unreported 6 August 1996, where the Scottish Court of Session endorsed a decision by the Panel to the effect that a solicitor who had been struck off the roll for six charges of dishonesty was not a suitable person to act on behalf of an appellant.)

11.10.1 Public funding for CICA claims

As stated at 7.4.1 above, it was mistakenly stated at paragraph 14.6.6 of *Criminal Injuries Compensation Claims* (Law Society, 2005) that there was no public funding for CICA claims save that in some circumstances legal aid can be obtained in respect of judicial review applications. In fact, there continues to be some limited public funding assistance available under the old 'Green Form' Scheme, but this would not ordinarily extend to the costs of representation.

11.11 CALCULATING TIME

There have not previously been any rules for the calculation of time expressly provided under the Schemes. In reality, and helpfully for most appellants, when a review decision is made the deadline by which the appeal must be submitted, i.e. within 90 days, has been and continues to be specified in bold at the end of the review decision. The rules clarify that the deadline for any date is 5 pm and that if any deadline is reached on other than a working day, e.g. a Sunday, then so long as the act required is done by the next working day, e.g. Monday, this will be deemed to have been done in time (rule 12(2)). A working day is any day except Saturday, Sunday or a bank holiday including Christmas Day and Good Friday.

11.12 SENDING AND DELIVERY OF DOCUMENTS

Service of documents may be effected by post, by hand, or by fax where there is a number specified for the proceedings (rule 13(1)) or as permitted or directed by the Tribunal. It should be noted that if a party provides a fax number, email address or other details for electronic transmission then 'that party must accept delivery of documents by that method' unless the party notifies all other parties that such a method may not be used (rule 13(2)). Equally, if a party informs the Tribunal or other parties that a particular form of communication (other than by hand or by pre-paid post) should not be used, then it should not be used (rule 13(3)). If an electronic means of communication has been used and the party wishes to have a hard copy they may request one but should do so as soon as reasonably practicable.

11.13 DISCLOSURE AND PUBLICITY IN RELATION TO PROCEEDINGS

Criminal injuries compensation hearings have always been held in private with the caveat that subject to the consent of the appellant, permission could be given for a hearing to be attended by members of the press or other observers. Permission was only ever granted on the basis that undertakings would be given to keep confidential the identity of the appellant and any other persons referred to unless that person consented and that no material would be disclosed or in any other way published without the consent of the subject. (This rule was formerly in the body of the older Schemes.) Rule 14 of the Tribunal Procedure Rules permits the Tribunal to regulate the use of documents and disclosure or publication of documents. It is a permissive power. However, this should be viewed in conjunction with rule 30 which provides that:

> (2) A hearing in a criminal injuries compensation case must be held in private unless –
>
> (a) the appellant has consented to the hearing being held in public; and
> (b) the Tribunal considers that it is in the interests of justice for the hearing to be held in public.

(3) The Tribunal may give a direction that a hearing, or part of it, is to be held in private.
(4) Where a hearing, or part of it, is to be held in private, the Tribunal may determine who is permitted to attend the hearing or part of it.

Therefore the position is preserved whereby criminal injuries hearings are held in private unless the appellant consents and the Tribunal considers that it is in the interests of justice for the hearing to be held in public. In reality there is nothing to prevent an appellant publishing the details of their claim after a hearing as long as they do not identify any other person involved in the proceedings without that person's consent to such publicity. For obvious reasons most appellants choose to retain their anonymity. This does mean that there are very few reported cases in respect of the application of the Schemes now that the annual reports from the Tribunal no longer contain examples of anonymised claims. Applicants and their advisers are now reliant largely on the few reported judicial review claims to gain additional guidance as to the application of the Schemes in practice. Practitioners will find useful case law with accompanying headnotes on the Tribunal's website at **www.cicap.gov.uk**.

11.13.1 Direction prohibiting disclosure

Turning back to rule 14, if one party wishes to keep a document confidential from another party on the ground that it would be likely to cause that person or some other person serious harm and, having regard to the interests of justice, it is proportionate to make such a direction, then the party can apply to the Tribunal for a direction to prohibit disclosure (rule 14(2)). An example of where this rule could be deployed could be an application by the CICA to suggest that information relating to the details of sexual abuse of a victim who was an infant at the time, not be disclosed if the victim had no memory of the abuse and may not have manifested any psychological signs or symptoms of having been abused and it may be more harmful than not to disclose the information. In those circumstances the CICA may run the case on the basis that it is not in the interests of the victim to make an award. There is a 'half-way house' provision whereby disclosure may be provided to the representative but not to the individual concerned. See rule 14(5) and (6) in this regard:

(5) If the Tribunal gives a direction under paragraph (2) which prevents disclosure to a party who has appointed a representative, the Tribunal may give a direction that the documents or information be disclosed to that representative if the Tribunal is satisfied that –

(a) disclosure to the representative would be in the interests of the party; and
(b) the representative will act in accordance with paragraph (6).

(6) Documents or information disclosed to a representative in accordance with a direction under paragraph (5) must not be disclosed either directly or indirectly to any other person without the Tribunal's consent.

This may be a useful tool in ensuring that the appellant is given informed advice as to his or her position and the merits of the claim in a way that would minimise the prospect of harm from damaging information.

11.14 EVIDENCE AND SUBMISSIONS

As set out above, rule 15 supplements the general case management powers available to the Tribunal and permits the Tribunal to give directions in respect of evidence and submissions and the provision of expert or lay witness evidence. The Tribunal and its predecessors have always had a very wide discretion in respect of the admissibility of evidence in whatever form it comes before it. It has always been possible to accept hearsay evidence tempered by appropriate considerations as to the weight it should be given. This practice is now formulated in rule 15 of the Tribunal Procedure Rules:

(2) The Tribunal may –

(a) admit evidence whether or not –

(i) the evidence would be admissible in a civil trial in the United Kingdom; or

(ii) the evidence was available to a previous decision maker; or

(b) exclude evidence that would otherwise be admissible where –

(i) the evidence was not provided within the time allowed by a direction or a practice direction;

The breadth of the general discretion previously applied appears to remain unfettered in that even evidence submitted late or in breach of a direction or practice direction may be admitted.

11.15 WITHDRAWAL OF APPEALS

There was no specific provision within the previous Schemes which permitted an appellant to withdraw an appeal. The position was that once the Panel was seized of an appeal, technically the review decision had been rejected and the Panel was bound to consider the matter afresh in light of all the evidence by then available unless it gave permission to the appellant to withdraw. Rule 17 provides that a notice of withdrawal will not take effect unless the Tribunal consents to the withdrawal (rule 17(2) and (3)). A notice of withdrawal may be given prior to a hearing or orally at the hearing (rule 17(1)). The reasoning behind this has always been to protect the public purse so that if the reason for the withdrawal related to new issues which had come to light such as further convictions or further evidence which adversely affected the prospects of the appeal, this could be taken into account. The Panel, and the Board before it, had a long tradition of warning appellants at the commencement of an appeal hearing if they considered it reasonably likely that the appellant would be worse off in pursuing the appeal (known in some circles as 'the canary warning') and, if they considered it equitable, allowing the appellant to withdraw at that stage. Under rule 17(4) a party who has withdrawn their case may apply to the Tribunal to have the appeal reinstated. They have a one-month time frame (from the date on which the Tribunal received the notice/heard the oral application) within which this may be done. There is no guidance within the rule as to the exercise of discretion in this regard.

11.16 PART 3: CHAPTER 2 – HEARINGS

Part 3 of the Tribunal Procedure Rules deals with hearings. In **Chapter 10** the substantive procedural rules in relation to making an appeal have been considered. This section examines the rest of the rules which supplement these.

11.16.1 Entitlement to attend a hearing

The appellant and the CICA have always been entitled, subject to the right to exclude in appropriate cases, to attend a hearing. Indeed appellants are expected to attend the hearing of their appeal and failure to do so is more likely to result in failure of the appeal than any other outcome. The 1996 and 2001 Schemes envisaged that appellants would attend although there was no express rule that they did so. This position is continued by rule 28 which provides:

> Subject to rule 30(5) (exclusion of a person from a hearing), each party to proceedings is entitled to attend a hearing.

It is tempered by the power in rule 30(5) and (6) to exclude persons because of their conduct:

> (5) The Tribunal may give a direction excluding from any hearing, or part of it –
>
> (a) any person whose conduct the Tribunal considers is disrupting or is likely to disrupt the hearing;
> (b) any person whose presence the Tribunal considers is likely to prevent another person from giving evidence or making submissions freely;
> (c) any person who the Tribunal considers should be excluded in order to give effect to a direction under rule 14(2) (withholding information likely to cause harm); or
> (d) any person where the purpose of the hearing would be defeated by the attendance of that person.
>
> (6) The Tribunal may give a direction excluding a witness from a hearing until that witness gives evidence.

This power as indicated above can be exercised in respect of parties or their witnesses or representatives.

11.16.2 Hearings in a party's absence

The 2001 Scheme provided that an appeal may be determined in the appellant's absence where the appellant had so requested or agreed or had given no reasonable excuse for failure to attend or was in custody or in hospital and likely to remain so for at least six months or was not living in Great Britain and it would not be against the interests of justice so to do (paragraph 78 of the 2001 Scheme). In such circumstances if the appeal proceeded the appellant could apply in writing for a re-hearing (paragraph 79). It should be noted that if a representative attended on the appellant's behalf then no application for a re-hearing could properly be made since one could not say that the appeal had been determined in the appellant's absence (*R (on the application of O'Neill)* v. *CICAP* [2002] EWHC 486 (Admin)). See further *R. (on the application of Riley)* v. *CICAP* [2008] EWHC 1954 (Admin) where the claimant had sustained a brain injury as a consequence of an assault. Notice of the listing for the appeal hearing had come in when the solicitor instructed was out of the jurisdiction and he could not attend the hearing which was listed just after he came back. The appellant had not attended because he considered he could not represent himself. The appeal was dismissed on the basis that there was a lack of evidence to show his injuries were directly attributable and because there was evidence that his conduct had contributed to the assault and further he had previous relevant convictions. An application for a re-hearing on the basis that he had been unable to represent himself was refused. Upon judicial review, the administrative court held that he could not reasonably have been expected to represent himself and there was probably little difference between him so doing or being absent. He did have a reasonable excuse and there was a real possibility that an injustice had occurred, therefore the application was granted. The new Tribunal Procedure Rules take a more simplistic approach as follows, under rule 31:

> If a party fails to attend a hearing the Tribunal may proceed with the hearing if the Tribunal –
>
> (a) is satisfied that the party has been notified of the hearing or that reasonable steps have been taken to notify the party of the hearing; and
> (b) considers that it is in the interests of justice to proceed with the hearing.

The position remains, therefore, that the Tribunal can proceed to hear the appeal in the absence of the appellant or his or her representative so long as the conditions above are fulfilled. However, there is a right to request a re-hearing pursuant to rule 37 which states:

> (1) The Tribunal may set aside a decision which disposes of proceedings, or part of such a decision, and re-make the decision, or the relevant part of it, if –
>
> (a) the Tribunal considers that it is in the interests of justice to do so; and
> (b) one or more of the conditions in paragraph (2) are satisfied.
>
> (2) The conditions are –
>
> [. . .]
> (c) a party, or a party's representative, was not present at a hearing related to the proceedings; or
> (d) there has been some other procedural irregularity in the proceedings.
>
> (3) A party applying for a decision, or part of a decision, to be set aside under paragraph (1) must make a written application to the Tribunal so that it is received no later than 1 month after the date on which the Tribunal sent notice of the decision to the party.

The appellant has one month from the date of the decision to get the application for a re-hearing to the Tribunal. There is no additional guidance as to the exercise of the discretion in determining whether or not to grant a re-hearing. The overriding objective will no doubt be applied. We suggest that the reasoning in the two cases cited above will still be relevant notwithstanding the change in the rules.

11.17 PART 3: CHAPTER 3 – DECISIONS

Rule 32 provides that the Tribunal may, at the request of the parties, if it considers it appropriate, make a consent order disposing of the proceedings. This is unlikely in a criminal injuries appeal unless it relates to directions which have been scrutinised by the Tribunal or an agreement to withdraw an appeal with which it is satisfied. Traditionally the decisions provided at the conclusion of an appeal hearing have been given orally (in the vast majority of cases). This tradition is continued by rule 33 which permits the Tribunal to give its decision orally. Representatives ought to make a careful note of the reasons given for the decision orally since unless they apply for written reasons subsequently this is their only chance to understand any findings of fact or the thinking behind the decision the Tribunal has reached. There is a further formality (consistent with the previous practice) in that pursuant to rule 33(2):

> Subject to rule 14(2) (withholding information likely to cause harm), the Tribunal must provide to each party as soon as reasonably practicable after making a decision which finally disposes of all issues in the proceedings (except a decision under Part 4) –
>
> (a) a decision notice stating the Tribunal's decision;
> (b) where appropriate, notification of the right to apply for a written statement of reasons under rule 34(3); and
> (c) notification of any right of appeal against the decision and the time within which, and the manner in which, such right of appeal may be exercised.

11.17.1 Written reasons

The previous informal practice which permitted a party to apply for written reasons is now embodied in rule 33(2)(b) above. In practice at the conclusion of the appeal hearing, generally a few minutes after the parties have withdrawn, the clerk will hand to the appellant or his or her representatives a 'decision sheet' which records the decision of the Tribunal. This will contain no reasons, merely the result.

11.18 FURTHER APPEAL ROUTES

It remains the case that, as under the old regime, there is strictly speaking no 'right of appeal' against any decision of the Tribunal save for judicial review proceedings where there has been an error of law. However, there are a number of distinct sets of circumstances where there is a right to a re-hearing or a right to apply for reinstatement. These are usefully summarised in the practice and guidance statement CI-6 'Appeals on errors of law against final decision of the Tribunal' (see **Appendix 4**) as to which see further below. Where a party is unhappy with the appeal decision and is considering the prospect of judicial review proceedings then they may make a written application to the Tribunal for a statement of reasons pursuant to rule 34(3). The application must be received by the Tribunal within one month of the date of the decision notice (rule 34(4)). There is now a deadline for the

Tribunal of one month from the date on which it received the application, or as soon as reasonably practicable after the end of that period, by which written reasons (if requested) ought to be supplied (rule 34(5)).

11.19 PART 4: CORRECTING, SETTING ASIDE, REVIEWING AND APPEALING TRIBUNAL DECISIONS

Part 4, as the title above suggests, deals with correcting, setting aside, reviewing and appealing Tribunal decisions. The first point to note is that the provisions which relate to clerical mistakes and setting aside decisions on specified grounds do apply to criminal injuries claims. However, the appeal provisions (rules 38 and 39) do not apply to criminal injuries claims. As intimated above the only true 'appeal route' from the Tribunal is an application for judicial review. The previous regime, therefore, has not substantially altered although we would suggest that there is more room now on the face of the rules to seek the setting aside of an appeal decision. Rules 36 and 37 are the relevant rules in so far as these claims are concerned.

11.19.1 Clerical mistakes

Rule 36 deals with clerical mistakes and accidental slips or omissions and provides as follows:

> The Tribunal may at any time correct any clerical mistake or other accidental slip or omission in a decision, direction or any document produced by it, by –
>
> (a) sending notification of the amended decision or direction, or a copy of the amended document, to all parties; and
> (b) making any necessary amendment to any information published in relation to the decision, direction or document.

There was previously no formal rule to this effect although parties could have made a request to the Chairman of the Panel or subsequently, the Principal Judge of the Tribunal to consider such a matter.

11.19.2 Setting aside decisions

Rule 37 is the more substantive rule which deals with setting aside a decision which disposes of proceedings. We have already considered this above in so far as it is relevant to the failure of an appellant or his or her representative to attend the appeal hearing. However, it bears repetition and provides:

> (1) The Tribunal may set aside a decision which disposes of proceedings, or part of such a decision, and re-make the decision, or the relevant part of it, if –
>
> (a) the Tribunal considers that it is in the interests of justice to do so; and
> (b) one or more of the conditions in paragraph (2) are satisfied.

(2) The conditions are –

(a) a document relating to the proceedings was not sent to, or was not received at an appropriate time by, a party or a party's representative;
(b) a document relating to the proceedings was not sent to the Tribunal at an appropriate time;
(c) a party, or a party's representative, was not present at a hearing related to the proceedings; or
(d) there has been some other procedural irregularity in the proceedings.

(3) A party applying for a decision, or part of a decision, to be set aside under paragraph (1) must make a written application to the Tribunal so that it is received no later than 1 month after the date on which the Tribunal sent notice of the decision to the party.

The pre-conditions to a successful application are therefore that the Tribunal considers that it is in the interests of justice to permit the setting aside of the decision and that there was: (a) some difficulty with service or documents or disclosure; or (b) a non-attendance by the appellant or his or her representative; or (c) there has been some 'other procedural irregularity' in the proceedings. On the face of it this should allow an appeal to be re-visited where, for example, a party has been taken by surprise by late disclosure/service of documents and the appeal went ahead, e.g. late disclosure of crucial police evidence (although it would have been incumbent on the Tribunal to consider any reasonable request for an adjournment). In terms of 'procedural irregularity' this may be concerned with the manner in which the hearing was performed. We are aware of one case under the old regime where a Chairman of the Panel appeared to have fallen asleep at one stage during the hearing! A re-hearing was subsequently granted in that case.

11.19.3 Guidance

The practice and guidance statement CI-6 'Appeals on errors of law against final decision of the Tribunal' (at **Appendix 4** to this book) contains a useful summary of the circumstances in which an appeal decision may be challenged and states:

> None of the tariff based Schemes and the Rules applicable to decisions made by the First-tier Tribunal in this jurisdiction provide for a final decision of the Tribunal to be reviewed, appealed, amended or otherwise interfered with, apart from
>
> (i) the right to apply for re-instatement (a) where proceedings, or part of them, have been struck out (Rule 8(5)-(7)) or (b) where proceedings or part of them have been withdrawn (Rule 17(4));
> (ii) the right to apply for a decision to be reconsidered at a hearing where the Tribunal makes a decision which disposes of proceedings without a hearing, other than decisions to which Rule 27(5) apply (Rule 27(4));
> (iii) the right to apply for a rehearing where the tribunal proceeded with a hearing in a party's absence (Rule 31);
> (iv) the correction of a clerical or other accidental slip or omission in a decision (Rule 36);
> (v) the right to apply for a decision, or part of a decision, to be set aside subject to certain conditions (Rule 37).

11.20 JUDICIAL REVIEW

As the practice guidance referred to above goes on to state, unless the appellant can bring his or her challenge within one of those prescribed criteria, the only solution would be judicial review. If the claim concerns an incident in England or Wales then the judicial review claim is directed to the Upper Tribunal (Administrative Appeals Chamber) located in central London or in Newport in Wales. If in Scotland the claim is directed to the Outer House of the Court of Session. The guidance note C1-6 (see Appendix 4) does give some useful practical information in respect of making a judicial review application and should be consulted closely by practitioners. The analysis of circumstances where an action for judicial review may be founded as set out in Chapter 20 of *Criminal Injuries Compensation Claims* (Law Society, 2005) is still relevant in this regard. Practitioners should be aware that the Tribunal is not represented at Judicial Review hearings. Its decision stands or falls as the judgment of a judge would.

Appendix 1
THE CRIMINAL INJURIES COMPENSATION SCHEME (2008)

Criminal Injuries Compensation Authority
Tay House, 300 Bath Street
GLASGOW G2 4LN
Freephone number: 0800 358 3601 Fax: 0141 331 2287
www.cica.gov.uk

TABLE OF CONTENTS

Standard amount of compensation
26. Tariff amount for listed injuries.
27. Multiple injuries.
28. Unlisted injuries.
29. Interim award for unlisted injuries.

Compensation for loss of earnings
30. Period of loss.
31. Past and future loss.
32. Multipliers, discount factors and life expectancy.
33. Alternative calculation of future loss.
34. Limit on rate of loss.

Compensation for special expenses
35. Types of special expenses.
36. Special expenses continuing at time of assessment.

Compensation in fatal cases
37. Funeral expenses.
38. Qualifying claimants.
39. Standard amount of compensation.
40. Dependency.
41. Calculation of dependency compensation.
42. Compensation for loss of parent.
43. Award to victim before death.
44. Supplementary compensation.

Effect on awards of other payments
45. Social security benefits and insurance payments.
46. Pensions.
47. Refusal of award pending claim.
48. Compensation and damages from other sources.
49. Repayment of award.

Determination of applications and payment of awards
50. Notification of award and arrangements for payment.
51. Lump sum and interim payments.
52. Purchase of annuities.

Reconsideration of decisions
53. Final payment not yet made.
54. Decision already notified to applicant.
55. Decision in accordance with direction by First-tier Tribunal.

Re-opening of cases
56. Change in victim's medical condition.
57. Time limit.

Review of decisions
58. Decisions open to review.
59. Written application within time limit.
60. Procedure on review.

Appeals
61. Right of appeal.
62. Appeal against refusal to re-open case.
63. Direction to Authority where appeal concerns time-limit or refusal to re-open.
64. Direction to Authority where appeal concerns award.
65. Further powers on appeal.

THE CRIMINAL INJURIES COMPENSATION SCHEME (2008)

1. This Scheme is made by the Secretary of State under the Criminal Injuries Compensation Act 1995. Applications received on or after 3 November 2008 for the payment of compensation to, or in respect of, persons who have sustained criminal injury will be considered under this Scheme (subject to paragraphs 66-70).

Administration of the Scheme

2. Claims officers in the Criminal Injuries Compensation Authority ('the Authority') will determine claims for compensation in accordance with this Scheme. Appeals against decisions taken on reviews under this Scheme will be determined by the First-tier Tribunal established under the Tribunals, Courts and Enforcement Act 2007.
3. Claims officers will be responsible for deciding, in accordance with this Scheme, what awards (if any) should be made in individual cases, and how they should be paid. Their decisions will be open to review and thereafter to appeal to the First-tier Tribunal, in accordance with this Scheme. No decision, whether by a claims officer or the First-tier Tribunal, will be open to appeal to the Secretary of State.
4. The general working of this Scheme will be kept under review by the Secretary of State.
5. The Accounting Officer for the Authority must submit a report to the Secretary of State and the Scottish Ministers as soon as possible after the end of each financial year, dealing with the operation of this Scheme and the discharge of functions under it. The Accounting Officer must keep proper accounts and proper records in relation to those accounts, and must prepare a statement of accounts in each financial year in a form directed by the Secretary of State. This statement of accounts must be submitted to the Secretary of State and the Scottish Ministers as soon as possible after the end of each financial year.

Eligibility to apply for compensation

6. Compensation may be paid in accordance with this Scheme:
   (a) to an applicant who has sustained a criminal injury on or after 1 August 1964;
   (b) where the victim of a criminal injury sustained on or after 1 August 1964 has since died, to an applicant who is a qualifying claimant for the purposes of paragraph 38 (compensation in fatal cases).

   For the purposes of this Scheme, 'applicant' means any person for whose benefit an application for compensation is made, even where it is made on his or her behalf by another person.

7. No compensation will be paid under this Scheme in the following circumstances:

   (a) where the applicant has previously lodged any claim for compensation in respect of the same criminal injury under this or any other scheme for the compensation of the victims of violent crime in operation in Great Britain; or
   (b) where the criminal injury was sustained before 1 October 1979 and the victim and the assailant were living together at the time as members of the same family.

8. For the purposes of this Scheme, 'criminal injury' means one or more personal injuries as described in paragraph 9, being an injury sustained in and directly attributable to an act occurring in Great Britain (see Note 1) which is:

   (a) a crime of violence (including arson, fire-raising or an act of poisoning); or
   (b) an offence of trespass on a railway; or
   (c) the apprehension or attempted apprehension of an offender or a suspected offender, the prevention or attempted prevention of an offence, or the giving of help to any constable who is engaged in any such activity.

9. For the purposes of this Scheme, personal injury includes physical injury (including fatal injury), mental injury (that is temporary mental anxiety, medically verified, or a disabling mental illness confirmed by psychiatric diagnosis) and disease (that is a medically recognised illness or condition). Mental injury or disease may either result directly from the physical injury or from a sexual offence or may occur without any physical injury. Compensation will not be payable for mental injury or disease without physical injury, or in respect of a sexual offence, unless the applicant:

   (a) was put in reasonable fear of immediate physical harm to his or her own person; or
   (b) had a close relationship of love and affection with another person at the time when that person sustained physical and/or mental injury (including fatal injury) directly attributable to conduct within paragraph 8(a), (b) or (c), and

      (i) that relationship still subsists (unless the victim has since died), and
      (ii) the applicant either witnessed and was present on the occasion when the other person sustained the injury, or was closely involved in its immediate aftermath; or

   (c) in a claim arising out of a sexual offence, was the non-consenting victim of that offence (which does not include a victim who consented in fact but was deemed in law not to have consented); or
   (d) being a person employed in the business of a railway, either witnessed and was present on the occasion when another person sustained physical (including fatal) injury directly attributable to an offence of trespass on a railway, or was closely involved in its immediate aftermath. Paragraph 12 does not apply where mental anxiety or mental illness is sustained as described in this sub-paragraph.

10. It is not necessary for the assailant to have been convicted of a criminal offence in connection with the injury. Moreover, even where the injury is attributable to conduct within paragraph 8 in respect of which the assailant cannot be convicted of an offence by reason of age, insanity or diplomatic immunity, the conduct may nevertheless be treated as constituting a criminal act.

11. A personal injury is not a criminal injury for the purposes of this Scheme where the injury is attributable to the use of a vehicle, except where the vehicle was used so as deliberately to inflict, or attempt to inflict, injury on any person. For the purposes of this Scheme a 'vehicle' is any device by which persons, animals or goods are or can be transported on or under land or water, or by air.

12. Where an injury is sustained accidentally by a person who is engaged in:

   (a) any of the law-enforcement activities described in paragraph 8(c), or

(b) any other activity directed to containing, limiting or remedying the consequences of a crime,

compensation will not be payable unless the person injured was, at the time he or she sustained the injury, taking an exceptional risk which was justified in all the circumstances.

Eligibility to receive compensation

13. (1) A claims officer may withhold or reduce an award where he or she considers that:

(a) the applicant failed to take, without delay, all reasonable steps to inform the police, or other body or person considered by the Authority to be appropriate for the purpose, of the circumstances giving rise to the injury; or

(b) the applicant failed to co-operate with the police or other authority in attempting to bring the assailant to justice; or

(c) the applicant has failed to give all reasonable assistance to the Authority or other body or person in connection with the application; or

(d) the conduct of the applicant before, during or after the incident giving rise to the application makes it inappropriate that a full award or any award at all be made; or

(e) the applicant's character as shown by his or her criminal convictions (excluding convictions spent under the Rehabilitation of Offenders Act 1974 at the date of application or death) or by evidence available to the claims officer makes it inappropriate that a full award or any award at all be made.

(2) No amount awarded in accordance with paragraph 35(1)(e), (f) or (g) (expenses associated with lack of mental capacity or trusts) will be reduced under sub-paragraph (1) above or under paragraph 14, unless the whole award is withheld under those provisions.

14. (1) In considering the issue of reasonable assistance under paragraph 13(1)(c), a claims officer may withhold an award where the applicant has repeatedly and without reasonable excuse failed to respond to the Authority's communications sent to his or her last known address.

(2) In considering the issue of conduct under paragraph 13(1)(d), a claims officer may withhold or reduce an award where he or she considers that excessive consumption of alcohol or use of illicit drugs by the applicant contributed to the circumstances which gave rise to the injury in such a way as to make it inappropriate that a full award, or any award at all, be made.

(3) In considering the issue of character under paragraph 13(1)(e), a claims officer must withhold or reduce an award to reflect unspent criminal convictions unless he or she considers that there are exceptional reasons not to do so.

15. Where the victim has died since sustaining the injury (whether or not in consequence of it), paragraphs 13 and 14 will apply in relation both to the deceased and to any applicant for compensation under paragraphs 37-44 (fatal awards).

16. A claims officer will make an award only where he or she is satisfied:

(a) that there is no likelihood that an assailant would benefit if an award were made; or

(b) where the applicant is under 18 years of age when the application is determined, that it would not be against his or her interest for an award to be made.

17. (1) Where a case is not ruled out under paragraph 7(b) (injury sustained before 1 October 1979) but at the time when the injury was sustained, the victim and

any assailant (whether or not that assailant actually inflicted the injury) were living in the same household as members of the same family, an award will be withheld unless:

(a) the assailant has been prosecuted in connection with the offence, or a claims officer considers that there are practical, technical or other good reasons why a prosecution has not been brought; and

(b) in the case of violence between adults in the family, a claims officer is satisfied that the applicant and the assailant stopped living in the same household before the application was made and are unlikely to share the same household again.

(2) For the purposes of this paragraph, a man and woman living together as husband and wife (whether or not they are married) or same sex partners living together (whether or not they are civil partners) will be treated as members of the same family.

(3) For the purposes of this Scheme, two people are 'civil partners' if they are civil partners for the purposes of the Civil Partnership Act 2004.

Consideration of applications

18. An application for compensation under this Scheme in respect of a criminal injury ('injury' hereafter in this Scheme) must be made in writing on a form obtainable from the Authority. It should be made as soon as possible after the incident giving rise to the injury and must be received by the Authority within two years of the date of the incident. A claims officer may waive this time limit only where he or she considers that:

(a) it is practicable for the application to be considered; and

(b) in the particular circumstances of the case, it would not have been reasonable to expect the applicant to have made an application within the two-year period.

19. (1) It will be for the applicant to make out his or her case including, where appropriate:

(a) making out the case for a waiver of the time limit in paragraph 18; and

(b) satisfying the claims officer dealing with the application (including an officer reviewing a decision under paragraph 60) that an award should not be reconsidered, withheld or reduced under any provision of this Scheme.

(2) Where an applicant is represented, the costs of representation will not be met by the Authority. Where an applicant incurs ancillary costs in making the application, such as a fee paid to an expert for a medical or other specialist report, these will not be met by the Authority unless they are met in accordance with paragraph 21 (medical examination of injury) or the claims officer otherwise considers that it is reasonable for the Authority to meet them, in full or in part.

20. A claims officer may make such directions and arrangements for the conduct of an application, including the imposition of conditions, as he or she considers appropriate in all the circumstances. The standard of proof to be applied by a claims officer in all matters will be the balance of probabilities.

21. Where a claims officer considers that an examination of the injury is required before a decision can be reached, the Authority will make arrangements for such an examination by a duly qualified medical practitioner. Reasonable expenses incurred by the applicant in that connection will be met by the Authority.

22. A Guide to the operation of this Scheme will be published by the Authority and will set out the procedures for dealing with applications.

Types and limits of compensation

23. Subject to the other provisions of this Scheme, the compensation payable under an award will be:

(a) a standard amount of compensation determined by reference to the nature of the injury in accordance with paragraphs 26-29;
(b) where the applicant has lost earnings or earning capacity for longer than 28 weeks as a direct consequence of the injury (other than injury leading to his or her death), an additional amount in respect of such loss of earnings, calculated in accordance with paragraphs 30-34;
(c) where the applicant has lost earnings or earning capacity for longer than 28 weeks as a direct consequence of the injury (other than injury leading to his or her death) or, if not normally employed, is incapacitated to a similar extent, an additional amount in respect of any special expenses, calculated in accordance with paragraphs 35-36;
(d) where the victim has died in consequence of the injury, the amount or amounts calculated in accordance with paragraphs 37-43;
(e) where the victim has died otherwise than in consequence of the injury, a supplementary amount calculated in accordance with paragraph 44.

24. The maximum award that may be made (before any reduction under paragraphs 13-15) in respect of the same injury will not exceed £500,000. For these purposes, where the victim has died in consequence of the injury, any application made by the victim before his or her death and any application made by any qualifying claimant or claimants after the victim's death will be regarded as being in respect of the same injury.
25. The injury, or any acceleration or exacerbation of a pre-existing condition, must be sufficiently serious to qualify for compensation equal at least to the minimum award under this Scheme in accordance with paragraph 26, but lesser compensation may be paid if an award is reduced under paragraph 13, 14, or 15.

Standard amount of compensation

26. The standard amount of compensation will be the amount shown in respect of the relevant description of injury in the Tariff, which sets out:

(a) a scale of fixed levels of compensation;
(b) the level and corresponding amount of compensation for each description of injury; and
(c) qualifying notes.

Level 1 represents the minimum award under this Scheme, and Level 25 represents the maximum award for any single description of injury. Where the injury has the effect of accelerating or exacerbating a pre-existing condition, the compensation awarded will reflect only the degree of acceleration or exacerbation.

27. Minor multiple injuries will be compensated in accordance with Note 12 to the Tariff. The standard amount of compensation for more serious but separate multiple injuries will, unless expressly provided for otherwise in the Tariff, be calculated as:

(a) the Tariff amount for the highest-rated description of injury; plus
(b) 30 per cent of the Tariff amount for the second highest-rated description of injury; plus, where there are three or more injuries,
(c) 15 per cent of the Tariff amount for the third highest-rated description of injury.

28. Where the Authority considers that any description of injury for which no provision is made in the Tariff is sufficiently serious to qualify for at least the minimum award under this Scheme, it will, following consultation with the First-tier Tribunal, refer the injury to the Secretary of State. In doing so the Authority will recommend to the Secretary of State both the inclusion of that description of injury in the Tariff and also the amount of compensation for which it should qualify. Any such consultation with the First-tier Tribunal or reference to the Secretary of State must not refer to the circumstances of any individual application for compensation under this Scheme other than the relevant medical reports.

29. Where an application for compensation is made in respect of an injury for which no provision is made in the Tariff and the Authority decides to refer the injury to the Secretary of State under paragraph 28, an interim award may be made of up to half the amount of compensation for which it is recommended that such description of injury should qualify if subsequently included in the Tariff. No part of such an interim award will be recoverable if the injury is not subsequently included in the Tariff or, if included, qualifies for less compensation than the interim award paid.

Compensation for loss of earnings

30. (1) Where the applicant has lost earnings or earning capacity for longer than 28 weeks as a direct consequence of the injury (other than injury leading to his or her death), no compensation in respect of loss of earnings or earning capacity will be payable for the first 28 weeks of loss. The period of loss for which compensation may be payable will begin after those 28 weeks and, subject to sub-paragraph (2) below, will continue for such period as a claims officer may determine.

(2) Where an injury has resulted in a reduction in the life expectancy of the applicant to an age below the applicant's expected retirement age, the period of loss for which compensation may be payable must be restricted to reflect that fact. No compensation in respect of loss of earnings or earning capacity will be payable in respect of any years of employment lost as a result of a reduction in life expectancy, subject to the right of a qualifying claimant to make an application for compensation under paragraphs 37-44 (compensation in fatal cases).

31. (1) Loss of earnings or earning capacity for any period of loss prior to the date of assessment (and, where appropriate, the date of the assessment itself) ('past loss'), will be assessed by:

(a) calculating the applicant's earnings as they would have been during the period of loss had it not been for the injury; and

(b) deducting any earnings which have, or should have, been paid to the applicant during the period of loss, whether or not as a result of the injury.

(2) Loss of earnings or earning capacity for any period of loss following the date of assessment ('future loss') will be assessed by:

(a) calculating in accordance with sub-paragraphs (1)(a) and (1)(b) above an annual rate of loss at the time of the assessment (the 'multiplicand'); and

(b) calculating any further multiplicand being such future annual rate of loss as the claims officer may determine taking into account his or her assessment of the applicant's likely future earnings and future earning capacity; and

(c) multiplying each multiplicand by an appropriate multiplier (and applying any other relevant factor) in accordance with paragraph 32.

(3) For the purposes of this Scheme, 'earnings' includes any profit or gain payable in respect of an office or employment (including salary, benefits in kind, pensions benefits (whether or not paid as a lump sum), redundancy payments and other severance payments) and will be calculated net of tax, national insurance and pension contributions.

32. The compensation payable in respect of each period of future loss will be a lump sum, which is the product of the relevant multiplicand and an appropriate multiplier. When the loss does not start until a future date, the lump sum will be discounted to provide for the present value of the money. The claims officer will assess the appropriate multiplier,

discount factor, or life expectancy by reference to the tables in Note 3, and may make such adjustments as he or she considers appropriate to take account of any factors and contingencies which appear to him or her to be relevant. The tables in Note 3 set out the multipliers and (where applicable) discounts and life expectancies to be applied.

(a) Table A is to be applied to various periods of future loss to allow for the accelerated receipt of compensation;
(b) Table B sets out the discount factor, by which the lump sum is to be multiplied, when the loss does not start until various periods in the future;
(c) Table C is a life expectancy table, and in the absence of other factors affecting life expectancy, the table sets out the age to be applied when assessing a multiplier based on pecuniary loss for life.

33. Where a claims officer considers that the approach in paragraphs 31 and 32 to assessing compensation for future loss of earnings or earning capacity is impracticable, the compensation payable in respect of that loss will be such other lump sum as he or she may determine.
34. Any rate of net loss of earnings or earning capacity (before any reduction in accordance with this Scheme) which is to be taken into account in calculating any compensation payable under paragraphs 30-33 must not exceed one and a half times the median gross weekly earnings at the time of assessment according to the latest figures published by the Office for National Statistics.

Compensation for special expenses

35. (1) Where the applicant has lost earnings or earning capacity for longer than 28 weeks as a direct consequence of the injury (other than injury leading to his or her death), or, if not normally employed, is incapacitated to a similar extent, additional compensation may be payable in respect of any special expenses incurred by the applicant from the date of the injury for:

(a) loss of or damage to property or equipment belonging to the applicant on which he or she relied as a physical aid, where the loss or damage was a direct consequence of the injury;
(b) costs (other than by way of loss of earnings or earning capacity) associated with National Health Service treatment for the injury;
(c) the cost of private health treatment for the injury, but only where a claims officer considers that, in all the circumstances, both the private treatment and its cost are reasonable;
(d) the reasonable cost, to the extent that it falls to the applicant, of

(i) special equipment, and/or
(ii) adaptations to the applicant's accommodation, and/or
(iii) care (in connection with the applicant's bodily functions or the preparation of meals) and supervision (to avoid substantial danger to the applicant or others), whether in a residential establishment or at home, which is not provided or available free of charge from the National Health Service, local authorities or any other agency, provided that a claims officer considers such expense to be necessary as a direct consequence of the injury;

(e) fees payable to the Public Guardian or the Court of Protection, or to any sheriff court in respect of an application made under the Adults with Incapacity (Scotland) Act 2000 (the '2000 Act');
(f) other costs associated with the administration of the applicant's affairs due to his or her lack of mental capacity (such as the costs of administering a power of attorney, the fees of a receiver or deputy appointed to act in a professional capacity, or the costs associated with a guardianship or

intervention order under the 2000 Act) provided that the claims officer considers that the costs were necessarily incurred as a result of the injury and are reasonable;

(g) the reasonable cost of setting up and administering a trust pursuant to a direction given by the claims officer under paragraph 50 (determination of applications and payment of awards).

(2) In the case of sub-paragraph (1)(d)(iii) above, the expense of unpaid care provided at home by a relative or friend of the victim will be compensated by having regard to the level of care required, the cost of a carer, assessing the carer's loss of earnings or earning capacity and/or additional personal and living expenses, as calculated on such basis as a claims officer considers appropriate in all the circumstances. Where the foregoing method of assessment is considered by the claims officer not to be relevant in all the circumstances, the compensation payable will be such sum as he or she may determine having regard to the level of care provided.

(3) For the purposes of this Scheme, the 'Court of Protection' includes the superior court of record created by section 45(1) of the Mental Capacity Act 2005 (the '2005 Act') and the office of the Supreme Court called the Court of Protection which ceased to exist under section 45(6) of that Act; and the 'Public Guardian' includes the officer appointed by the Lord Chancellor under section 57 of the 2005 Act and the Public Guardian established under section 6 of the 2000 Act.

36. (1) Where, at the time the claim is assessed, a claims officer is satisfied that the need for any of the special expenses mentioned in paragraph 35, other than special equipment, is likely to continue, the claims officer will determine the annual cost and select an appropriate multiplier in accordance with paragraph 32 (multipliers, discount factors and life expectancy), taking account of any other factors and contingencies which appear to him or her to be relevant.

(2) Where, at the time the claim is assessed, a claims officer is satisfied that the need for special equipment is likely to continue and that the equipment will require replacement on occasions in the future, the claims officer will calculate the replacement value at each date of replacement, being the cost of the new equipment less the sale value of the old equipment, and select an appropriate discount factor in accordance with paragraph 32 (multipliers, discount factors and life expectancy) taking account of any other factors and contingencies which appear to him or her to be relevant.

Compensation in fatal cases

37. Where the victim has died in consequence of the injury, no compensation other than funeral expenses will be payable for the benefit of his or her estate. Such expenses will, subject to the application of paragraphs 13 and 14 in relation to the actions, conduct and character of the deceased, be payable up to an amount considered reasonable by a claims officer, even where the person bearing the cost of the funeral is otherwise ineligible to claim under this Scheme.

38. (1) Where the victim has died:

(a) if the death was in consequence of the injury, compensation may be payable to a qualifying claimant under paragraphs 39-43 (standard amount of compensation, dependency, and loss of parent); or

(b) if the death was otherwise than in consequence of the injury, and occurred before title to the award had been vested in the victim (see paragraph 50), compensation may be payable to a qualifying claimant under paragraph 44 (supplementary compensation), and no standard amount or other compensation will be payable to the estate or to the qualifying claimant other than under that paragraph.

(2) A 'qualifying claimant' is a person who at the time of the deceased's death was:

(a) the partner of the deceased, being only, for these purposes:

(i) a person who was living together with the deceased as husband and wife or as a same sex partner in the same household (or a person who would have been so living but for infirmity or ill health preventing physical proximity in the same house) immediately before the date of death and who, unless married to that person or a civil partner of that person, had been so living throughout the two years before that date, or

(ii) a spouse or civil partner or former spouse or civil partner of the deceased who was financially supported by the deceased immediately before the date of death; or

(b) a natural parent of the deceased, or a person who was not the natural parent but was accepted by the deceased as a parent within the deceased's family; or

(c) a natural child of the deceased, or a person who was not the natural child but was accepted by the deceased as a child within the deceased's family or was dependent on the deceased.

But a person who was criminally responsible for the death of a victim may not be a qualifying claimant.

Where victim died in consequence of injury

39. A qualifying claimant may claim an award under this paragraph (a 'bereavement award') unless he or she was a former spouse or civil partner of the deceased or was otherwise estranged from the deceased immediately before the date of death. In cases where only one person qualifies for a bereavement award, the standard amount of compensation will be Level 13 of the Tariff, save that where a claims officer is aware of the existence of one or more other persons who would in the event of their making a claim qualify for a bereavement award, the standard amount of compensation will be Level 10 of the Tariff. Where more than one person qualifies for a bereavement award, the standard amount of compensation for each claimant will be Level 10 of the Tariff.

40. (1) Additional compensation calculated in accordance with paragraph 41 may be payable to a qualifying claimant where a claims officer is satisfied that the claimant was financially or physically dependent on the deceased. A financial dependency will not be established where the deceased's only normal income was from social security benefits.

(2) For the purposes of this Scheme, 'social security benefits' includes all United Kingdom social security benefits, other state or local authority benefits and all such benefits or similar payments paid from the funds of other countries.

41. The amount of compensation payable in respect of dependency will be calculated on a basis similar to paragraphs 31-34 (loss of earnings) and paragraph 35(1)(d)(iii) (cost of care). The period of loss will begin from the date of the deceased's death and continue for such period as a claims officer may determine, with no account being taken, where the qualifying claimant was married to or a civil partner of the deceased, of remarriage or prospects of remarriage or of a new civil partnership or the prospects of a new civil partnership. In assessing the dependency, the claims officer will take account of the qualifying claimant's earnings and other income, if any. Where the deceased had been living in the same household as the qualifying claimant before death, the claims officer will, in calculating the multiplicand, make such proportional reduction as he or she considers appropriate to take account of the deceased's own personal and living expenses.

42. Where a qualifying claimant was under 18 years of age at the time of the deceased's death and was dependent on the deceased for parental services, the following additional compensation may also be payable:
    (a) a payment for loss of that parent's services at an annual rate of Level 5 of the Tariff; and
    (b) such other payments as a claims officer considers reasonable to meet other resultant losses.

    Each of these payments will be multiplied by an appropriate multiplier selected by a claims officer in accordance with paragraph 32 (multipliers, discount factors and life expectancy), taking account of the period remaining before the qualifying claimant reaches age 18 and of any other factors and contingencies which appear to the claims officer to be relevant.

43. Application may be made under paragraphs 37-42 (compensation in fatal cases) even where an award had been made to the victim in respect of the same injury before his or her death. Any such application will be subject to the conditions set out in paragraphs 56-57 for the re-opening of cases, and any compensation payable to the qualifying claimant or claimants, except payments made under paragraphs 37 and 39 (funeral expenses and standard amount of compensation), will be reduced by the amount paid to the victim. The amounts payable to the victim and the qualifying claimant or claimants will not in total exceed £500,000.

Where victim died otherwise than in consequence of injury

44. Where a victim who would have qualified for additional compensation under paragraph 23(b) (loss of earnings) and/or paragraph 23(c) (special expenses) has died, otherwise than in consequence of the injury, before such compensation was awarded, supplementary compensation under this paragraph may be payable to a qualifying claimant who was financially dependent on the deceased within the terms of paragraph 40 (dependency), whether or not a relevant application was made by the victim before his or her death. Payment may be made in accordance with paragraph 31(1) in respect of the victim's loss of earnings (except for the first 28 weeks of the victim's loss of earnings and/or earnings capacity) and in accordance with paragraph 35 in respect of any special expenses incurred by the victim before his or her death. The amounts payable to the victim and the qualifying claimant or claimants will not in total exceed £500,000.

Effect on awards of other payments

45. (1) The compensation payable to an applicant under this Scheme, other than compensation payable under paragraphs 26, 27, 39 and 42(a) (tariff-based amounts of compensation), will be reduced to take account of any social security benefits or insurance payments made by way of compensation for the same contingency.
    (2) No reduction under this paragraph will be made to take account of an insurance payment if it is made under an insurance arrangement entered into and wholly funded by the victim personally (or by the parent or guardian of a victim who was under the age of 18 at the time of the injury), except where the reduction is made to compensation payable under paragraph 35(1)(c), (d), (e) or (f) (subject, if appropriate, to paragraph 36).
    (3) Subject to sub-paragraph (4) below, a reduction under this paragraph will be made irrespective of the period in respect of which the social security benefits or insurance payments have been, or will be paid. In particular, the reduction will be made whether or not any actual loss occurred or will occur in that period.
    (4) No reduction under this paragraph will be made to take account of any social security benefits or insurance payments paid in respect of the first 28 weeks of lost earnings.

(5) Subject to sub-paragraph (6) below, the amount of the reduction will be the full value of the social security benefits or insurance payments less the amount of any income tax which has been or may be charged in respect of them.

(6) If the benefits or payments will be paid after the date of the assessment, the claims officer will calculate the amount of the reduction as he or she would calculate a lump sum to compensate for future loss under paragraph 32 (multipliers, discount factors and life expectancy).

(7) For the purposes of this Scheme, disablement pension payable under section 103 of the Social Security Contributions and Benefits Act 1992 will be treated as a social security benefit payable to compensate for loss of earnings, loss of earning capacity or loss of pension benefits.

46. (1) Where the victim is alive, any compensation payable under paragraphs 30-34 (loss of earnings) will be reduced to take account of any pension benefits accruing as a result of the injury which have not already been taken into account in calculations under those paragraphs. Where the victim has died in consequence of the injury, any compensation payable under paragraphs 40-41 (dependency) will similarly be reduced to take account of any pension benefits which have not already been taken into account in calculations under those paragraphs and which are payable, as a result of the victim's death, for the benefit of the applicant.

(2) For the purposes of this paragraph, 'pension benefits' means any payment payable as a result of the injury or death in pursuance of pension or any other rights connected with the victim's employment, and includes any gratuity of that kind and similar benefits payable under insurance policies paid for by the victim's employers. Pension rights accruing solely as a result of payments by the victim or a dependant will be disregarded.

(3) Subject to sub-paragraph (4) below, a reduction under this paragraph will be made irrespective of the period in respect of which the pension benefits have been, or will be paid. In particular, a reduction will be made whether or not any actual loss of earnings or earning capacity occurred or will occur in that period.

(4) No reduction under this paragraph will be made to take account of any pension benefits paid in respect of the first 28 weeks of lost earnings.

(5) Subject to sub-paragraph (6) below, where such pension benefits are taxable, one half of their gross value will be deducted, but they will otherwise be deducted in full (where, for example, a lump sum payment not subject to income tax is made).

(6) If the pension benefits will be paid after the date of the assessment, the claims officer will calculate the amount of the reduction as he or she would calculate a lump sum to compensate for future loss under paragraph 32 (multipliers, discount factors and life expectancy). In the case of taxable pension benefits the claims officer will assume for these purposes that the applicant will receive one half of their gross value.

47. Where, in the opinion of a claims officer, an applicant may be or may become eligible for any social security benefits, insurance payments or pension benefits, within the meaning of paragraph 45 or 46, an award may be withheld until the applicant has taken such steps as the claims officer considers reasonable to claim them.

48. (1) An award payable under this Scheme will be reduced by the full value of any payment in respect of the same injury which the applicant has received or to which he or she has any present or future entitlement, as a result of:

(a) any criminal injury compensation award made under or pursuant to arrangements in force at the relevant time in Northern Ireland;

(b) any compensation award or similar payment from the funds of a country or other territory outside the United Kingdom;

(c) an order by a civil court whether in the United Kingdom or elsewhere for the payment of damages;
(d) an order by a criminal court whether in the United Kingdom or elsewhere for payment of compensation in respect of personal injuries or a compensation offer under section 302A of the Criminal Procedure (Scotland) Act 1995; or
(e) a settlement of a claim for damages, compensation or both on terms providing for the payment of money.

(2) In calculating reductions under this paragraph, the full value of a payment listed in sub-paragraph (1) above is the payment less the amount of any benefits which are recoverable under the Social Security (Recovery of Benefits) Act 1997, or under any equivalent legislation in Northern Ireland or a country or territory outside the United Kingdom.

(3) A claims officer may require an applicant to provide details of any steps taken or planned to obtain damages or compensation in respect of the same injury and may decline to process an application further until those details have been provided or until the applicant's attempts to obtain such damages or compensation have been exhausted.

49. (1) Where a person in whose favour an award under this Scheme is made subsequently receives any other payment in respect of the same injury in any of the circumstances mentioned in paragraph 48, but the award made under this Scheme was not reduced accordingly, the person will be required to repay the Authority in full up to the amount of the other payment.

(2) Any monies received by the Authority under sub-paragraph (1) above that relate to criminal injuries sustained otherwise than in Scotland shall be paid to the Secretary of State and any such monies that relate to criminal injuries sustained in Scotland shall be paid to the Scottish Ministers.

Determination of applications and payment of awards

50. (1) An application for compensation under this Scheme will be determined by a claims officer, and written notification of the decision will be sent to the applicant or the applicant's representative. Written acceptance of an award must be received by the Authority within 90 days of the date the decision was issued. If such an acceptance is not received within that period, and no application for a review under paragraph 59 has been made, the Authority may withdraw the award. A claims officer may grant an extension to this time limit (whether or not it has already expired) and overturn any withdrawal, if:

(a) the applicant has made a written request for an extension; and
(b) the claims officer considers that there are exceptional circumstances which justify the granting of an extension.

(2) The claims officer may make such directions and arrangements, including the imposition of conditions, in connection with the acceptance, settlement, or trust, payment, repayment and/or administration of an award as he or she considers appropriate in all the circumstances. Any such directions and arrangements, including any settlement or trust may be made having regard to the interests of the applicant (whether or not a minor or a person under an incapacity) as well as to considerations of public policy (including the desirability of providing for the return of any parts of an award which may prove to be surplus to the purposes for which they were awarded) on terms which do not exhaust the beneficial interest in the award and which provide, either expressly or by operation of law, for the balance of any trust fund to revert to the Authority. Subject to any such arrangements, including the special procedures in paragraph 52 (purchase of annuities), and to paragraphs 53-55 (reconsideration of

decisions), title to an award offered will be vested in the applicant when the Authority has received notification in writing that the applicant accepts the award.

51. Compensation will normally be paid as a single lump sum, but one or more interim payments may be made where a claims officer considers this appropriate. Once an award has been paid to an applicant or the applicant's representative, paragraph 52 does not apply.
52. Where prior agreement is reached between the Authority and the applicant or the applicant's representative, an award may consist in whole or in part of an annuity or annuities, purchased for the benefit of the applicant or to be held on trust for his or her benefit. Once that agreement is reached, the Authority will take the instructions of the applicant or the applicant's representative as to which annuity or annuities should be purchased. Any expenses incurred will be met from the award.

Reconsideration of decisions

53. A decision made by a claims officer (other than a decision made in accordance with a direction by the First-tier Tribunal on determining an appeal under paragraph 64) may be reconsidered at any time before actual payment of a final award where there is new evidence or a change in circumstances. In particular, the fact that an interim payment has been made does not preclude a claims officer from reconsidering issues of eligibility for an award.
54. Where an applicant has already been sent written notification of the decision on the application, the applicant will be sent written notice that the decision is to be reconsidered, and any representations which the applicant sends to the Authority within 30 days of the date of such notice will be taken into account in reconsidering the decision. Whether or not any such representations are made, the applicant will be sent written notification of the outcome of the reconsideration, and where the original decision is not confirmed, such notification will include the revised decision.
55. Where a decision to make an award has been made by a claims officer in accordance with a direction by the First-tier Tribunal on determining an appeal under paragraph 64, but before the award has been paid the claims officer considers that there is new evidence or a change in circumstances which justifies reconsidering whether the award should be withheld or the amount of compensation reduced, the Authority will refer the case to the First-tier Tribunal for rehearing.

Re-opening of cases

56. A decision made by a claims officer and accepted by the applicant, or a direction by the First-tier Tribunal, will normally be regarded as final, except where an appeal is reheard. A claims officer may, however, subsequently re-open a case where there has been such a material change in the victim's medical condition that injustice would occur if the original assessment of compensation were allowed to stand, or where the victim has since died in consequence of the injury.
57. A case will not be re-opened more than two years after the date of the final decision unless the claims officer is satisfied, on the basis of evidence presented in support of the application to re-open the case, that the renewed application can be considered without a need for further extensive enquiries.

Review of decisions

58. (1) An applicant may seek a review of any decision under this Scheme by a claims officer:

    (a) not to waive or extend the time limit in paragraph 18 (application for compensation) or paragraph 59 (application for review); or

(b) not to re-open a case under paragraphs 56-57; or
(c) to withhold an award, including such decision made on reconsideration of an award under paragraphs 53-54; or
(d) to make an award, including a decision to make a reduced award whether or not on reconsideration of an award under paragraphs 53-54; or
(e) to require repayment of an award under paragraph 49; or
(f) to withdraw an award under paragraph 50(1).

(2) An applicant may not, however, seek the review of any such decision:

(a) where the decision was itself made on a review under paragraph 60 and either the applicant did not appeal against it or the appeal did not result in a direction from the First-tier Tribunal; or
(b) where the decision was made in accordance with a direction by the First-tier Tribunal on determining an appeal under paragraph 64.

59. An application for the review of a decision by a claims officer must be made in writing to the Authority and must be supported by reasons together with any relevant additional information. It must be received by the Authority within 90 days of the date the decision to be reviewed was issued. However, a claims officer other than the one who made the original decision may grant an extension to this time limit (whether or not it has already expired) if:

(a) the applicant has made a written request for an extension; and
(b) the claims officer considers that there are exceptional circumstances which justify the granting of an extension.

60. (1) All applications for review will be considered by a claims officer other than the one who made the original decision. The officer conducting the review will reach a decision in accordance with the provisions of this Scheme applying to the original application, and will not be bound by any earlier decision either as to the eligibility of the applicant for an award or as to the amount of an award. The applicant will be sent written notification of the outcome of the review, giving reasons for the review decision, and the Authority will, unless it receives notice of an appeal, ensure that a determination of the original application is made in accordance with the review decision.

(2) Where, on review of a decision not to re-open a case under paragraphs 56-57, the reviewing claims officer decides to re-open the case, he or she will proceed to determine the application for compensation. If the applicant is dissatisfied with that determination, he or she may appeal under paragraph 61.

Appeals

61. An applicant who is dissatisfied with a decision taken on a review under paragraph 60(1) or with a determination under paragraph 60(2) may appeal against the decision to the First-tier Tribunal in accordance with Tribunal Procedure Rules.

62. Where the appeal concerns a decision not to re-open a case under paragraphs 56-57, and the application for re-opening was made more than two years after the date of the final decision, the First-tier Tribunal must be satisfied that the renewed application can be considered without a need for further extensive enquiries by the Authority.

63. (1) Where the First-tier Tribunal allows an appeal against a decision taken on review under paragraph 58(1)(a), (b) or (f), it will direct the Authority in accordance with this paragraph.

(2) In a case where the appeal was against a decision not to waive the time limit in paragraph 18, the First-tier Tribunal will direct the Authority to arrange for the application for compensation to be dealt with under this Scheme as if the time limit had been waived by a claims officer.

(3) In a case where the appeal was against a decision not to extend the time limit in

paragraph 59, the First-tier Tribunal will direct the Authority to conduct a review under paragraph 60.

(4) In a case where the appeal was against a decision not to re-open a case, the First-tier Tribunal will direct the Authority to re-open the case under paragraphs 56-57.

(5) In a case where the appeal was against a decision to withdraw an award under paragraph 50(1), the First-tier Tribunal will direct the Authority to allow the applicant a further period of 90 days in which either to accept the award or seek a review on other grounds.

64. Where the First-tier Tribunal allows an appeal against a decision taken on review under paragraph 58(1)(c), (d) or (e) it will make such direction as it thinks appropriate as to the decision to be made by a claims officer on the application for compensation, but any such direction must be in accordance with the relevant provisions of this Scheme.

65. The First-tier Tribunal also has the following powers when determining an appeal against a decision taken on review under paragraph 58(1)(c), (d) or (e):

(a) on application or adjournment the First-tier Tribunal may direct that an interim payment be made; and

(b) where an appeal is found to be frivolous or vexatious, the First-tier Tribunal may reduce the amount of compensation to be awarded by such amount as it considers appropriate.

Implementation and transitional provisions

66. The provisions of this Scheme come into force on 3 November 2008. All applications for compensation received by the Authority on or after 3 November 2008 will be dealt with under the terms of this Scheme, except that in relation to applications in respect of injuries incurred before 1 April 2001 paragraph 38 of this Scheme shall not apply, but only insofar as it applies to a same sex partner.

67. Applications for compensation received by the Authority or by the Criminal Injuries Compensation Board ('the Board') before 3 November 2008 will continue to be dealt with:

(a) if they were received on or after 1 April 2001, in accordance with the provisions of the scheme which came into operation on 1 April 2001 ('the 2001 Scheme') as modified by paragraph 68 of this Scheme; or

(b) if they were received on or after 1 April 1996 but before 1 April 2001, in accordance with the provisions of the scheme which came into operation on 1 April 1996 ('the 1996 Scheme') as modified by the 2001 Scheme and by paragraph 68 of this Scheme; or

(c) if they were received before 1 April 1996, in accordance with the provisions of the non-statutory scheme which came into operation on 1 February 1990 ('the old Scheme'). This includes provisions of the earlier non-statutory schemes referred to therein, insofar as they continue to have effect immediately before 3 November 2008 by virtue of the 1996 or 2001 Schemes or the provisions of any non-statutory scheme.

68. Where an application is required by paragraph 67 to be dealt with under the 1996 Scheme or the 2001 Scheme, with effect from 3 November 2008 any appeal against a decision taken on review will be to the First-tier Tribunal and will be dealt with in accordance with Tribunal Procedure Rules (subject to any transitional arrangements).

69. From 3 November 2008 applications required by paragraph 67 to be dealt with according to the provisions of the old Scheme will continue to be so dealt with by the Authority, and any decision authorised under the old Scheme to be made by one or more members of the Board may be made by the First-tier Tribunal.

70. Cases which are reopened under paragraph 56 of this Scheme or any corresponding provision of any earlier scheme will be dealt with according to the terms of the scheme under which the initial application was decided, subject to paragraphs 68 and 69 of this Scheme.

NOTES TO THE SCHEME

(see paragraph 8)

Note 1 – Definition of Great Britain

(a) For the purposes of paragraph 8 of this Scheme, an injury is sustained in Great Britain where it is sustained:

- (i) on a British aircraft, hovercraft or ship (see Note 2); or
- (ii) on, under or above an installation in a designated area within the meaning of section 1(7) of the Continental Shelf Act 1964 or any waters within 500 metres of such an installation; or
- (iii) in a lighthouse off the coast of Great Britain.

(b) For the purposes of paragraph 8 of this Scheme –

- (i) an injury is sustained in Great Britain where it is sustained in that part of the Channel Tunnel system incorporated into England under section 10 of the Channel Tunnel Act 1987. However, if such an injury is sustained or caused by a non-UK officer acting in the exercise of his or her functions under the 1993 and 1994 Orders no compensation shall be payable under this Scheme; and
- (ii) any injury caused in the following circumstances shall be treated for the purposes of any application for compensation under this Scheme as if the circumstances giving rise to the claim had occurred in Great Britain –
  - (a) an injury sustained by a UK officer acting in the exercise of his or her functions within French or Belgian territory under the provisions of the 1993 and 1994 Orders; or
  - (b) an injury caused by a UK officer acting in the exercise of those functions within French or Belgian territory, other than an injury to any non-UK officer acting in the exercise of his or her functions.

In this Note 'the 1993 and 1994 Orders' mean the Channel Tunnel (International Arrangements) Order 1993 (SI 1993/1813) and the Channel Tunnel (Miscellaneous Provisions) Order 1994 (SI 1994/1405) and 'officer' has the same meaning as in those Orders.

Note 2 – Definitions of British aircraft, British hovercraft and British ship

In Note 1 above:

(a) 'British aircraft' means a British controlled aircraft within the meaning of section 92 of the Civil Aviation Act 1982 (application of criminal law to aircraft), or one of Her Majesty's aircraft;

(b) 'British hovercraft' means a British controlled hovercraft within the meaning of that section (as applied in relation to hovercraft by virtue of provision made under the Hovercraft Act 1968), or one of Her Majesty's hovercraft; and

(c) 'British ship' means one of Her Majesty's Ships or any vessel used in navigation which is owned wholly by persons of the following descriptions, namely:

- (i) British citizens, or
- (ii) bodies corporate incorporated under the law of some part of, and having their principal place of business in, the United Kingdom, or
- (iii) Scottish partnerships.

The references in this Note to Her Majesty's aircraft, hovercraft or ships are references to aircraft, hovercraft or ships which belong to, or are exclusively used in the service of, Her Majesty in right of the government of the United Kingdom or the Scottish Administration.

Note 3 – Multipliers and Discount Factors for assessing accelerated receipt of compensation, and life expectancy table.

(See paragraph 32)

Table A

(This converts an annual loss over a period of years into a lump sum payable at the beginning of that period)

Years of loss	*Multiplier*	*Years of loss*	*Multiplier*
5	5	17	11.5
6	5.5	18	12
7	6	19	12.5
8	7	20	13
9	7.5	25	15
10	8	30	16
11	8.5	35	17
12	9	40	18
13	9.5	50	20
14	10		
15	10.5		
16	11		

Table B – Discount Factors

Period of Years	*Discount in Future*	*Period of years in Future*	*Discount*
5	0.80	17	0.48
6	0.77	18	0.46
7	0.74	19	0.44
8	0.71	20	0.42
9	0.68	25	0.34
10	0.65	30	0.27
11	0.62	35	0.22

Period of Years	*Discount in Future*	*Period of years in Future*	*Discount*
12	0.59	40	0.18
13	0.57	50	0.12
14	0.54		
15	0.52		
16	0.50		

Table C – Life expectancy table

Age at date of Assessment	*Age to which expected to live for purposes of calculation:*	
	Males	*Females*
0–25	80 years of age	84 years of age
26–50	81	84
51–60	81	85
61–65	82	85
66–70	83	86
71–73	84	87
74–76	85	87
77–78	86	88
79–80	87	89
81	88	89
82	88	90
83	89	90
84–85	90	91
86	91	92
87–88	92	93
89	93	94
90	94	95

CRIMINAL INJURIES COMPENSATION SCHEME

Levels of compensation	
Level 1	£1,000
Level 2	£1,250
Level 3	£1,500
Level 4	£1,750
Level 5	£2,000
Level 6	£2,500
Level 7	£3,300
Level 8	£3,800
Level 9	£4,400
Level 10	£5,500
Level 11	£6,600
Level 12	£8,200
Level 13	£11,000
Level 14	£13,500
Level 15	£16,500
Level 16	£19,000
Level 17	£22,000
Level 18	£27,000
Level 19	£33,000
Level 20	£44,000
Level 21	£55,000
Level 22	£82,000
Level 23	£110,000
Level 24	£175,000
Level 25	£250,000

INDEX TO TARIFF OF INJURIES [PAGE NUMBERS EDITED FOR THIS APPENDIX]

		Page Number
Head & neck	Burns	[109–10]
	Scarring	[110]
	Brain damage	[110–12]
	Ear	[112–13]
	Eye	[113–15]
	Face	[115–16]
	Neck	[116]
	Nose	[116]
	Skull	[117]
	Teeth	[117]
	Tongue	[117–18]
Upper limbs	Burns	[118]
	Scarring	[118]
	Arm	[118]
	Elbow	[118]
	Finger & Thumb	[119–20]
	Hand	[120]
	Humerus (upper arm bone)	[121]
	Radius (a forearm bone)	[121]
	Shoulder	[121]
	Tendon and/or Ligament and/or Cartilage	[122]
	Ulna (a forearm bone)	[122]
	Wrist	[123]

		Page Number
Torso	Burns	[123]
	Scarring	[123]
	Abdomen	[124]
	Back	[124]
	Chest	[125]
	Clavicle (collar bone)	[125]
	Coccyx (tail bone)	[125]
	Genitalia	[125]
	Hernia	[125]
	Kidney	[125]
	Lung	[125–6]
	Pancreas	[126]
	Pelvis	[126]
	Penetrating injury not otherwise compensated	[126]
	Rib	[126]
	Scapula (shoulder blade)	[126]
	Spleen	[126]
	Sternum (breast bone)	[126–7]
Lower limbs	Burns	[127]
	Scarring	[127]
	Ankle	[127]
	Femur (thigh bone)	[127–8]
	Fibula (lower leg bone)	[128]
	Foot	[128]
	Heel	[128–9]
	Hip	[129]
	Knee	[129]
	Leg	[130]
	Tendon and/or Ligament and/or Cartilage	[130]
	Tibia (shin bone)	[131]
	Toe	[131–2]

GENERAL NOTES TO TARIFF OF INJURIES

(Notes 1–3 follow paragraph 70 of the Scheme)

Note 4

Where the tariff compensates for an operation the award includes provision for the normal operation scarring.

Note 5

When a person suffers both a physical injury and a mental injury, and the tariff amount for the physical injury is higher than that for the mental injury, the applicant will be entitled only to the tariff amount for the physical injury.

When a person suffers both a physical injury and a mental injury, and the tariff amount for the mental injury is the same as or higher than that for the physical injury, the applicant will be entitled to awards for the separate injuries in accordance with paragraph 27 of the Scheme (the serious multiple injury formula).

When a person is a victim of a sexual offence and also suffers a mental injury, the applicant will be entitled only to whichever is the higher of the two tariff amounts.

TARIFF OF INJURIES

Description of injury	*Level*	*Standard Amount £*
GENERAL		
Fatal injury		
One qualifying claimant	13	11,000
Each qualifying claimant	10	5,500
Burns *Note 6. For other burn injuries see under individual parts of the body.*		
Affecting multiple areas of body covering over 25% of skin area, with significant scarring	19	33,000
Infection with HIV/Hepatitis B/Hepatitis C *Note 7. Not subject to the multiple injuries formula and may be paid in addition to other awards.*		
Infection with HIV/Hepatitis B/Hepatitis C	17	22,000
Loss of foetus	10	5,500
Major paralysis		
Hemiplegia (paralysis of one side of the body)	21	55,000
Paraplegia (paralysis of lower limbs)	24	175,000
Quadriplegia/tetraplegia (paralysis of all four limbs)	25	250,000

Description of injury	*Level*	*Standard Amount £*
Medically recognised illness/condition – not mental illness		
Moderately disabling disorder where the symptoms and disability persist for more than 6 weeks from the incident/date of onset		
– lasting 6 to 13 weeks	1	1,000
– lasting up to 28 weeks	5	2,000
– lasting over 28 weeks		
– – not permanent	7	3,300
– – permanent	12	8,200
Seriously disabling disorder where the symptoms and disability persist for more than 6 weeks from the incident/date of onset		
– lasting 6 to 13 weeks	5	2,000
– lasting up to 28 weeks	9	4,400
– lasting over 28 weeks		
– – not permanent	12	8,200
– – permanent	17	22,000

Mental illness and temporary mental anxiety

Notes:
8. Mental illness includes conditions attributed to post-traumatic stress disorder, depression and similar generic terms within which there may be:
(a) such psychological symptoms as anxiety, tension, insomnia, irritability, loss of confidence, agoraphobia and preoccupation with thoughts of guilt or self-harm; and
(b) related physical symptoms such as alopecia, asthma, eczema, enuresis and psoriasis.
9. 'Medically verified' means that the mental anxiety has been diagnosed by a registered medical practitioner.
10. 'Psychiatric diagnosis/prognosis' means that the disabling mental illness has been diagnosed or the prognosis made by a psychiatrist or clinical psychologist.
11. Mental anxiety or a mental illness is disabling if it significantly impairs a person's functioning in some important aspect of her/his life e.g. impaired work or school performance or significant adverse effects on social relationships or sexual dysfunction.

Description of injury	*Level*	*Standard Amount £*
Disabling but temporary mental anxiety lasting more than 6 weeks, medically verified	1	1,000
Disabling mental illness, confirmed by psychiatric diagnosis:		
– lasting up to 28 weeks	6	2,500
– lasting over 28 weeks to 2 years	9	4,400
– lasting 2 years to 5 years	12	8,200
– lasting over 5 years but not permanent	14	13,500
Permanent mental illness, confirmed by psychiatric prognosis		
– moderately disabling	16	19,000
– seriously disabling	18	27,000
Minor injuries: multiple		
Note 12: Minor multiple physical injuries will qualify for compensation only where the applicant has sustained at least 3 separate physical injuries of the type illustrated below, at least one of which must still have had significant residual effects 6 weeks after the incident. The injuries must also have necessitated at least 2 visits to or by a medical practitioner within that 6-week period. Examples of qualifying injuries are: *(a) grazing, cuts, lacerations (no permanent scarring)* *(b) severe and widespread bruising* *(c) severe soft tissue injury (no permanent disability)* *(d) black eye(s)* *(e) bloody nose* *(f) hair pulled from scalp* *(g) loss of fingernail*		
Minor injuries: multiple	1	1,000
Peripheral sensory nerve damage		
– lasting more than 13 weeks		
– – substantial recovery expected	3	1,500
– permanent disability		
– – minor loss	3	1,500
– – significant loss (eg loss of sensation in large area of leg)	7	3,300
– – serious loss (eg loss of sensation of hand)	12	8,200

Description of injury	*Level*	*Standard Amount £*
Peripheral motor nerve damage not otherwise compensated for		
– lasting more than 13 weeks		
– – substantial recovery expected	5	2,000
– permanent disability		
– – minor (eg paralysis or equivalent functional loss of finger/toe)	6	2,500
– – significant (eg paralysis or equivalent loss of handgrip/foot movement	12	8,200
Physical abuse of adults		
Note 13: In the case of adult applicants where there has been a series of assaults (sexual and/or physical) over a period of time, it may be that an applicant will qualify for compensation only for the single most recent incident, if in relation to the earlier incidents she/he failed to report them to the police without delay and/or failed to co-operate with the police in bringing the assailant to justice. Where the applicant is entitled to compensation for the series of assaults, she/he will qualify for an award as the victim of a pattern of abuse, rather than for a separate award for each incident.		
Serious abuse		
– intermittent physical assaults resulting in an accumulation of healed wounds, burns or scalds, but with no appreciable disfigurement	5	2,000
Severe abuse		
– pattern of repetitive violence resulting in minor disfigurement	10	5,500
Persistent pattern of severe abuse over a period exceeding 3 years	12	8,200
Physical abuse of children		
Minor abuse		
– isolated or intermittent assault(s) resulting in weals, hair pulled from scalp etc.	1	1,000
Serious abuse		
– intermittent physical assaults resulting in an accumulation of healed wounds, burns or scalds, but with no appreciable disfigurement	5	2,000

Description of injury	*Level*	*Standard Amount £*
Severe abuse		
– persistent pattern of repetitive violence resulting in:		
– – moderate multiple injuries (eg bruising and minor fractures) and/or minor disfigurement	10	5,500
– – significant multiple injuries	12	8,200
– – severe multiple injuries	14	13,500
Sexual offence where victim is any age (if not already compensated as a child)		
Note 14: Note 13 (under Physical Abuse of Adults) applies here too		
Sexual assault		
– minor – non-penetrative sexual physical act/or acts over clothing	1	1,000
– serious – non-penetrative sexual physical act/or acts under clothing	5	2,000
– severe – non-penile penetrative and/or oral-genital act or acts	7	3,300
– pattern of repetitive frequent severe abuse (whether by one or more attackers) over a period		
– – up to 3 years	11	6,600
– – exceeding 3 years	12	8,200
– resulting in serious internal bodily injuries	17	22,000
– resulting in permanently disabling mental illness confirmed by psychiatric prognosis	18	27,000
Non-consensual penile penetration of the vagina and/or anus and/or mouth		
– by one attacker	13	11,000
– by two or more attackers	14	13,500
– resulting in serious internal bodily injuries	17	22,000
– resulting in permanently disabling mental illness confirmed by psychiatric prognosis		
– – moderate mental illness	17	22,000
– – severe mental illness	18	27,000

Description of injury	*Level*	*Standard Amount £*
– resulting in serious internal bodily injury with permanent disabling mental illness confirmed by psychiatric prognosis		
– moderate mental illness	19	33,000
– severe mental illness	20	44,000
– pattern of repetitive incidents (whether by one or more attackers) over a period		
– up to 3 years	15	16,500
– exceeding 3 years	17	22,000
Sexual offence where victim is a child (under age of 18 at time or commencement of offence) or an adult who by reason of mental incapacity is incapable of giving consent		
Sexual assault		
– minor – non-penetrative sexual physical act/or acts over clothing	1	1,000
– minor – non-penetrative frequent sexual physical act/or acts over clothing	3	1,500
– serious – non-penetrative sexual physical act/or acts under clothing	5	2,000
– serious – pattern of repetitive non-penetrative sexual physical acts under clothing	7	3,300
Sexual assault		
– non-penile penetrative and/or oral genital act/or acts		
– one incident	7	3,300
– two or more isolated incidents	9	4,400
– pattern of repetitive, frequent incidents		
– over a period up to 3 years	11	6,600
– over a period exceeding 3 years	12	8,200
– resulting in serious internal bodily injuries	17	22,000
– resulting in permanently disabling mental illness confirmed by psychiatric prognosis		
– moderate mental illness	17	22,000

Description of injury	*Level*	*Standard Amount £*
– severe mental illness	18	27,000
Non-consensual penile penetration of the vagina and/or anus and/or mouth		
– one incident	13	11,000
– one incident involving two or more attackers	14	13,500
– repeated incidents over a period		
– up to 3 years	15	16,500
– exceeding 3 years	17	22,000
– resulting in serious internal bodily injuries	17	22,000
– resulting in permanently disabling mental illness confirmed by psychiatric prognosis		
– moderate mental illness	17	22,000
– severe mental illness	18	27,000
– resulting in serious internal bodily injury with permanent disabling mental illness confirmed by psychiatric prognosis		
– moderate mental illness	19	33,000
– severe mental illness	20	44,000
Sexual offences – additional awards where the following are directly attributable to a sexual offence (whether victim is an adult or a child) – not subject to the multiple injuries formula and may be paid in addition to other awards		
Pregnancy	10	5,500
Sexually transmitted disease other than HIV/Hepatitis B/Hepatitis C		
– substantial recovery	10	5,500
– permanent disability	13	11,000
Infection with HIV/Hepatitis B/Hepatitis C	17	22,000
HEAD & NECK		
Burns		
Head		
– minor visible disfigurement	5	2,000
– moderate	9	4,400
– severe	15	16,500

Description of injury		*Level*	*Standard Amount £*
Face			
–	minor disfigurement	5	2,000
–	moderate	10	5,500
–	severe	18	27,000
Neck			
–	minor disfigurement	3	1,500
–	moderate	9	4,400
–	severe	15	16,500
Scarring			
Head			
–	minor visible disfigurement	3	1,500
–	significant disfigurement	7	3,300
–	serious disfigurement	1	5,500
Face			
–	minor disfigurement	3	1,500
–	significant disfigurement	9	4,400
–	serious disfigurement	13	11,000
Neck			
–	minor disfigurement	3	1,500
–	significant disfigurement	7	3,300
–	serious disfigurement	11	6,600

Brain Damage

Note 15. A brain injury can cause physical and/or mental damage, resulting in, for example, spasticity, loss of balance, incontinence, or impairment of concentration, memory, motivation or personality. It can also commonly cause epilepsy, to a greater or lesser extent. Where the cause if any injury is brain damage there will not be additional awards for separate injuries but the seriousness of the combined effects will be measured together.

Minor head injury

Brain injury, if any, minimal. Concussion/impairment of balance/headaches			
–	lasting 6 to 28 weeks	3	1,500

Description of injury	*Level*	*Standard Amount £*
– lasting over 28 weeks	7	3,300
– permanent	12	8,200
Minor brain damage		
Good recovery, able to socialise and return to work but persisting problems with concentration, memory, disinhibition of mood affecting lifestyle, leisure activities, future work prospects		
– slight and short lived (6 months)	12	8,200
– moderate and medium term (2 years)	15	16,500
– significant and long lasting (more than 2 years)	17	22,000
Moderate brain damage		
Some dependence on others, intellectual deficit, personality change, ability to work reduced, some effect on the senses		
– slight	18	27,000
– moderate	21	55,000
– significant	22	82,000
Moderately severe brain damage		
Serious disablement of physical or mental faculties requiring substantial dependence on professional or other care, with marked impairment of intellect and personality, abnormal behaviour and poor communication	23	110,000
Very serious brain injury		
Severe physical limitation, significant effect on the senses with little insight and/or significant reduction in life expectancy. Little or no response to the environment, little or no language function, double incontinence and need for full-time/all day and some night nursing care	24	175,000
Note 16. Applications otherwise within level 25 fall into level 24 if life expectancy is greatly reduced and/or there is little or no insight as in a persistent vegetative state.		
No useful physical movement, significant effect on the senses and with some degree of insight. Little or no meaningful response to the environment, little or no language function, double incontinence and need for full-time nursing care.	25	250,000

Description of injury	*Level*	*Standard Amount £*
Epilepsy		
– post-traumatic epileptic fits – substantial recovery	5	2,000
– well controlled on medication	12	8,200
– partially controlled on medication	14	13,500
– uncontrolled despite medication	20	44,000
Ear		
Fractured mastoid	1	1,000
Deafness		
– temporary partial deafness		
– – lasting 6 to 13 weeks	1	1,000
– – lasting more than 13 weeks	3	1,500
– partial deafness (remaining hearing socially useful, with hearing aid if necessary)		
– – one ear	8	3,800
– – both ears	12	8,200
– total deafness		
– – one ear	15	16,500
– – in only hearing ear	19	33,000
– – both ears	20	44,000
Loss of ear		
– partial loss of ear(s)	9	4,400
– loss of ear	13	11,000
– loss of both ears	16	19,000
Perforated ear drum		
– one ear	4	1,750
– both ears	6	2,500
Tinnitus (ringing noise in ear(s))		
– lasting 6 to 13 weeks	1	1,000
– lasting more than 13 weeks	7	3,300
– permanent		
– – other than very severe	12	8,200

Description of injury	*Level*	*Standard Amount £*
– very severe	15	16,500
Vestibular damage (causing giddiness)		
– lasting 6 to 28 weeks	3	1,500
– lasting over 28 weeks – recovery expected	7	3,300
– permanent	12	8,200
Eye		
Blow out or other fracture of orbital bone cavity containing eyeball		
– no operation	7	3,300
– requiring operation	9	4,400
Blurred or double vision		
– temporary		
– lasting 6 to 13 weeks	1	1,000
– lasting more than 13 weeks – recovery expected	4	1,750
– permanent		
– slight	9	4,400
– moderate	12	8,200
– serious	14	13,500
Cataracts		
– one eye		
– requiring operation	7	3,300
– permanent/inoperable	12	8,200
– both eyes		
– requiring operation	12	8,200
– permanent/inoperable	16	19,000
Corneal abrasions	5	2,000
Permanent loss of visual field		
– slight	6	2,500
– moderate	10	5,500
– serious	20	44,000
Dislocation of lens		

Description of injury	*Level*	*Standard Amount £*
– one eye	10	5,500
– both eyes	14	13,500
Glaucoma	6	2,500
Hyphaema requiring operation		
– one eye	3	1,500
– both eyes	6	2,500
Loss of eye		
– one eye	18	27,000
– both eyes	23	110,000
Loss of sight		
– one eye	17	22,000
– one eye, where the sight in the uninjured eye cannot be corrected to better than 6/36	19	33,000
– one eye, where the uninjured eye is already totally blind	22	82,000
– both eyes	23	110,000
Partial loss of vision when corrected by glasses or contact lenses or other means e.g. laser surgery		
– better than 6/12	6	2,500
– 6/12	11	6,600
– 6/18	12	8,200
– 6/24	14	13,500
– 6/36	15	16,500
– 6/60	16	19,000
– substantial loss of vision (both eyes) at least 6/36 in each eye or worse	21	55,000
Residual central floater(s) affecting vision	7	3,300
Retina		
– damage not involving detachment		
– – one eye	6	2,500
– – both eyes	10	5,500
– detached		
– – one eye	10	5,500

Description of injury	*Level*	*Standard Amount £*
– both eyes	14	13,500
Significant penetrating injury		
– one eye	6	2,500
– both eyes	11	6,600
Traumatic angle recession	6	2,500
Face		
Clicking jaw		
– temporary		
– lasting 6 to 13 weeks	1	1,000
– lasting more than 13 weeks	3	1,500
– permanent	10	5,500
Dislocated jaw		
– substantial recovery	5	2,000
– continuing significant disability	10	5,500
Fractured ethmoid		
– no operation	5	2,000
– operation required	9	4,400
Fractured zygoma (malar/cheek bone)		
– no operation		
– substantial recovery	5	2,000
– continuing significant disability	9	4,400
– operation required		
– substantial recovery	6	2,500
– continuing significant disability	10	5,500
Fractured mandible and/or maxilla (jaw bones)		
– no operation		
– substantial recovery	7	3,300
– continuing significant disability	10	5,500
– operation required		
– substantial recovery	8	3,800
– continuing significant disability	12	8,200

Description of injury	*Level*	*Standard Amount £*
Multiple fractures to face (e.g. Le Fort fractures types 2 & 3)	13	11,000
Numbness/loss of feeling		
– temporary lasting more than 13 weeks – recovery expected	3	1,500
– permanent		
– – moderate eg cheek, forehead	7	3,300
– – severe eg lip interfering with function	9	4,400
Neck		
Fractured hyoid (bone in windpipe)	1	1,000
Strained neck or whiplash injury		
– disabling		
– – for 6 to 13 weeks	1	1,000
– – for more than 13 weeks	6	2,500
– seriously disabling		
– – not permanent	10	5,500
– – permanent	13	11,000
Nose		
Deviated nasal septum		
– no operation	1	1,000
– requiring septoplasty	5	2,000
Fracture of nasal bones		
– undisplaced	1	1,000
– displaced	3	1,500
– – requiring manipulation	5	2,000
– – requiring rhinoplasty	5	2,000
– – requiring turbinectomy	5	2,000
Loss of smell/taste		
– partial loss of smell and/or taste	10	5,500
– total		
– – loss of smell or taste	13	11,000
– – loss of smell and taste	15	16,500

Description of injury	*Level*	*Standard Amount £*
Partial loss of nose (at least 10%)	9	4,400
Skull		
Fracture		
– simple		
– – no operation	6	2,500
– – requiring operation	10	5,500
– depressed		
– – no operation	9	4,400
– – requiring operation	11	6,600
Teeth		
Damage to:		
– tooth/teeth requiring root-canal treatment	5	2,000
– front tooth/teeth requiring crown(s)	6	2,500
Fractured/chipped tooth/teeth requiring treatment	5	2,000
Fractured tooth/teeth requiring apicectomy (surgery to gum to reach root – root resection)	8	3,800
Loss of:		
– crowns	6	2,500
– front tooth/teeth (incisor or canine)		
– – one front tooth	7	3,300
– – two or three front teeth	9	4,400
– – four or more front teeth	10	5,500
– tooth/teeth other than front		
– – one tooth	5	2,000
– – two or more teeth	7	3,300
Slackening of teeth requiring dental treatment	5	2,000
Tongue		
Impaired speech		
– slight	5	2,000
– moderate	10	5,500
– serious	13	11,000
– severe	16	19,000

Description of injury			*Level*	*Standard Amount £*
	Loss of speech – permanent		19	33,000
	Loss of tongue		20	44,000
UPPER LIMBS				
Burns				
	Minor		3	1,500
	Moderate		9	4,400
	Severe		13	11,000
Scarring				
	Minor disfigurement		2	1,250
	Significant disfigurement		6	2,500
	Serious disfigurement		10	5,500
Arm				
	Loss of:			
	–	one non-dominant arm	19	33,000
	–	one dominant arm	21	55,000
	–	one arm where there is no remaining arm/hand with any useful function	22	82,000
	–	both arms	23	110,000
	Paralysis of or equivalent loss of function of:			
	–	one non-dominant arm	18	27,000
	–	one dominant arm	20	40,000
	–	total loss of function of one arm where there is no remaining arm/hand with any useful function	22	82,000
	–	both arms	22	82,000
Elbow				
	Dislocated/fractured			
	–	one elbow		
		– substantial recovery	7	3,300
		– continuing significant disability	12	8,200
	–	both elbows		
		– substantial recovery	12	8,200
		– continuing significant disability	13	11,000

Description of injury	*Level*	*Standard Amount £*
Finger and Thumb		
Fracture/dislocation of:		
– thumb		
– one hand		
– substantial recovery	5	2,000
– continuing significant disability	9	4,400
– both hands		
– substantial recovery	10	5,500
– continuing significant disability	12	8,200
– index finger		
– one hand		
– substantial recovery	4	1,750
– continuing significant disability	8	3,800
– both hands		
– substantial recovery	9	4,400
– continuing significant disability	11	6,600
– one finger other than index finger		
– one hand		
– substantial recovery	1	1,000
– continuing significant disability	5	2,000
– both hands		
– substantial recovery	4	1,750
– continuing significant disability	9	4,400
– two or more fingers other than index finger		
– one hand		
– substantial recovery	2	1,250
– continuing significant disability	6	2,500
– both hands		
– substantial recovery	7	3,300
– continuing significant disability	11	6,600

Description of injury	*Level*	*Standard Amount £*
Loss of:		
– finger other than index finger	10	5,500
– two or more fingers	13	11,000
– index finger	12	8,200
– both index fingers	15	16,500
– thumb	15	16,500
– both thumbs	21	55,000
Partial loss of:		
– finger other than thumb or index finger	6	2,500
– two or more fingers other than index finger or thumb	10	5,500
– thumb or index finger	9	4,400
– thumb or index finger – both hands	12	8,200
– thumb and index finger – one hand	12	8,200
– thumb and index finger – both hands	15	16,500
Hand		
Fractured hand		
– one hand		
– – substantial recovery	5	2,000
– – continuing significant disability	10	5,500
– both hands		
– – substantial recovery	8	3,800
– – continuing significant disability	12	8,200
Loss of, or equivalent loss of function of:		
– one non-dominant hand	19	33,000
– one dominant hand	21	55,000
– loss of, or total loss of function of one hand where there is no remaining hand/arm with any useful function	22	82,000
– both hands	23	110,000
Permanently & seriously impaired grip		
– one hand	12	8,200
– both hands	15	16,500

Description of injury	*Level*	*Standard Amount £*
Humerus (upper arm bone)		
Fractured		
– one arm		
– substantial recovery	7	3,300
– continuing significant disability	10	5,500
– both arms		
– substantial recovery	12	8,200
– continuing significant disability	13	11,000
Radius (a forearm bone)		
Fractured		
– one arm		
– substantial recovery	7	3,300
– continuing significant disability	10	5,500
– both arms		
– substantial recovery	12	8,200
– continuing significant disability	13	11,000
Shoulder		
Dislocated		
– one shoulder		
– substantial recovery	4	1,750
– continuing significant disability	10	5,500
– both shoulders		
– substantial recovery	8	3,800
– continuing significant disability	12	8,200
Frozen		
– one shoulder		
– substantial recovery	5	2,000
– continuing significant disability	10	5,500
– both shoulders		
– substantial recovery	7	3,300
– continuing significant disability	12	8,200

Description of injury	*Level*	*Standard Amount £*
Arthroscopy – where the shoulder is not dislocated, frozen or otherwise provided for	5	2,000
Tendon and/or Ligament and/or Cartilage		
Minor damage		
– one arm		
– substantial recovery	1	1,000
– continuing significant disability	6	2,500
– both arms		
– substantial recovery	5	2,000
– continuing significant disability	9	4,400
Moderate damage		
– one arm		
– substantial recovery	5	2,000
– continuing significant disability	9	4,400
– both arms		
– substantial recovery	9	4,400
– continuing significant disability	12	8,200
Severely damaged		
– one arm		
– substantial recovery	7	3,300
– continuing significant disability	10	5,500
– both arms		
– substantial recovery	11	6,600
– continuing significant disability	13	11,000
Ulna (a forearm bone)		
Fractured		
– one arm		
– substantial recovery	7	3,300
– continuing significant disability	10	5,500
– both arms		
– substantial recovery	12	8,200
– continuing significant disability	13	11,000

Description of injury	*Level*	*Standard Amount £*
Wrist		
Fractured – colles type or equivalent fracture/displacement of distal radius		
– one wrist		
– substantial recovery	9	4,400
– continuing significant disability	12	8,200
– both wrists		
– substantial recovery	12	8,200
– continuing significant disability	13	11,000
Fractured/dislocated – including scaphoid fracture		
– one wrist		
– substantial recovery	9	4,400
– continuing significant disability	12	8,200
– both wrists		
– substantial recovery	12	8,200
– continuing significant disability	13	11,000
Sprained		
– one wrist		
– disabling for 6 to 13 weeks	1	1,000
– disabling for more than 13 weeks	6	2,500
– both wrists		
– disabling for 6 to 13 weeks	5	2,000
– disabling for more than 13 weeks	8	3,800
TORSO		
Burns		
Minor	3	1,500
Moderate	9	4,400
Severe	13	11,000
Scarring		
Minor disfigurement	2	1,250
Significant disfigurement	6	2,500
Serious disfigurement	10	5,500

Description of injury	*Level*	*Standard Amount £*
Abdomen		
Injury requiring laparoscopy – including no repair or repair of one organ	5	2,000
Injury requiring laparotomy – including no repair or repair of one organ	8	3,800
Injury requiring laparotomy/laparoscopy		
– including repair of two organs	10	5,500
– including repair of three or more organs	12	8,200
Laparotomy with colostomy and/or ileostomy and/or ureterostomy lasting more than 14 weeks but not permanent	10	5,500
Laparotomy with permanent colostomy and/or ileostomy and/or ureterostomy	14	13,500
Back		
Fracture of vertebra		
– one vertebra		
– – substantial recovery	6	2,500
– – continuing significant disability	10	5,500
– more than one vertebra		
– – substantial recovery	9	4,400
– – continuing significant disability	12	8,200
Prolapsed invertebral disc(s)		
– seriously disabling		
– – not permanent	10	5,500
– – permanent	12	8,200
Ruptured invertebral disc(s) – requiring surgical removal	13	11,000
Strained		
– disabling		
– – for 6 to 13 weeks	1	1,000
– – for more than 13 weeks	6	2,500
– seriously disabling		
– – not permanent	10	5,500
– – permanent	13	11,000

Description of injury	*Level*	*Standard Amount £*
Chest		
Injury requiring thoracotomy	12	8,200
Injury requiring thoracotomy with removal/extensive repair of organ or organs	15	16,500
Clavicle (collar bone)		
Dislocated acromioclavicular joint	5	2,000
Fractured		
– one clavicle		
– – substantial recovery	5	2,000
– – continuing significant disability	9	4,400
– two clavicles		
– – substantial recovery	9	4,400
– – continuing significant disability	11	6,600
Coccyx (tail bone)		
Fractured	6	2,500
Genitalia		
Injury requiring medical treatment		
– no significant permanent damage	4	1,750
– permanent damage		
– – moderate	10	5,500
– – severe	13	11,000
Loss of fertility	21	55,000
Hernia		
– hernia	8	3,800
– hernias	10	5,500
Kidney		
Loss of kidney	13	11,000
Serious and permanent damage to or loss of both or only functioning kidney	21	55,000
Lung		
Punctured		
– one lung	7	3,300

Description of injury	*Level*	*Standard Amount £*
– both lungs	11	6,600
Collapsed		
– one lung	8	3,800
– both lungs	12	8,200
Permanent and disabling damage to lungs from smoke or chemical inhalation	13	11,000
Pancreas		
Loss of pancreas	15	16,500
Pelvis		
Fractured		
– substantial recovery	9	4,400
– continuing significant disability	13	11,000
Penetrating injury not otherwise compensated		
Symptoms persisting for at least a week	1	1,000
Rib		
Fractured (or bruised where significant pain lasts more than 6 weeks)		
– one rib	1	1,000
– two or more	3	1,500
Scapula (shoulder blade)		
Fractured		
– one scapula		
– – substantial recovery	6	2,500
– – continuing significant disability	9	4,400
– both scapulas		
– – substantial recovery	9	4,400
– – continuing significant disability	11	6,600
Spleen		
Loss of spleen	13	11,000
Sternum (breast bone)		
Fractured		
– substantial recovery	6	2,500

Description of injury	*Level*	*Standard Amount £*
– continuing significant disability	10	5,500
LOWER LIMBS		
Burns		
Minor	3	1,500
Moderate	9	4,400
Severe	13	11,000
Scarring		
Minor disfigurement	2	1,250
Significant disfigurement	6	2,500
Serious disfigurement	10	5,500
Ankle		
Fractured or Dislocated		
– one ankle		
– substantial recovery	9	4,400
– continuing significant disability	13	11,000
– both ankles		
– substantial recovery	12	8,200
– continuing significant disability	15	16,500
Sprained		
– one ankle		
– disabling for at least 6 to 13 weeks	1	1,000
– disabling for more than 13 weeks	6	2,500
– both ankles		
– disabling for at least 6 to 13 weeks	5	2,000
– disabling for more than 13 weeks	8	3,800
Femur (thigh bone)		
Fractured		
– one leg		
– substantial recovery	8	3,800
– continuing significant disability	11	6,600
– both legs		

Description of injury	*Level*	*Standard Amount £*
– substantial recovery	10	5,500
– continuing significant disability	13	11,000
Fibula (slender bone from knee to ankle)		
Fractured		
– one leg		
– substantial recovery	6	2,500
– continuing significant disability	8	3,800
– both legs		
– substantial recovery	7	3,300
– continuing significant disability	10	5,500
Foot		
Fractured metatarsal bones		
– one foot		
– substantial recovery	6	2,500
– continuing significant disability	8	3,800
– both feet		
– substantial recovery	7	3,300
– continuing significant disability	10	5,500
Fractured tarsal bones		
– one foot		
– substantial recovery	7	3,300
– continuing significant disability	12	8,200
– both feet		
– substantial recovery	10	5,500
– continuing significant disability	14	13,500
Heel		
Fractured heel bone		
– one foot		
– substantial recovery	7	3,300
– continuing significant disability	12	8,200
– both feet		

Description of injury	*Level*	*Standard Amount £*
– – substantial recovery	10	5,500
– – continuing significant disability	14	13,500
Hip		
Fractured/Dislocated		
– one hip		
– – substantial recovery	9	4,400
– – continuing significant disability	13	11,000
– both hips		
– – substantial recovery	12	8,200
– – continuing significant disability	15	16,500
Knee		
Arthroscopy (investigative surgery / repair to knee) – no fracture	5	2,000
Patella (knee cap)		
– Dislocated		
– – one knee		
– – – substantial recovery	1	1,000
– – – continuing significant disability	10	5,500
– – both knees		
– – – substantial recovery	6	2,500
– – – continuing significant disability	12	8,200
– Fractured		
– – one knee		
– – – substantial recovery	6	2,500
– – – continuing significant disability	10	5,500
– – both knees		
– – – substantial recovery	9	4,400
– – – continuing significant disability	12	8,200
removal of		
– one knee	8	3,800
– both knees	10	5,500

Description of injury	*Level*	*Standard Amount £*
Leg		
Loss of		
– one leg		
– – below knee	19	33,000
– – above knee	20	44,000
– loss of, or total loss of function of one leg where there is no remaining leg with useful function	22	82,000
– both legs, whether below or above knee	23	110,000
Paralysis of leg (see also major paralysis {paraplegia})	18	27,000
Tendon and/or Ligament and/or Cartilage		
Minor damage		
– one leg		
– – substantial recovery	1	1,000
– – continuing significant disability	7	3,300
– both legs		
– – substantial recovery	5	2,000
– – continuing significant disability	10	5,500
Moderate damage		
– one leg		
– – substantial recovery	5	2,000
– – continuing significant disability	10	5,500
– both legs		
– – substantial recovery	9	4,400
– – continuing significant disability	13	11,000
Severe damage		
– one leg		
– – substantial recovery	7	3,300
– – continuing significant disability	12	8,200
– both legs		
– – substantial recovery	11	6,600
– – continuing significant disability	15	16,500

Description of injury	*Level*	*Standard Amount £*
Tibia (shin bone)		
Fractured		
– one leg		
– – substantial recovery	8	3,800
– – continuing significant disability	11	6,600
– both legs		
– – substantial recovery	10	5,500
– – continuing significant disability	13	11,000
Toe		
Fractured		
– great toe		
– – one foot		
– – – substantial recovery	6	2,500
– – – continuing significant disability	12	8,200
– – both feet		
– – – substantial recovery	8	3,800
– – – continuing significant disability	14	13,500
– two or more toes		
– – one foot		
– – – substantial recovery	1	1,000
– – – continuing significant disability	6	2,500
– – both feet		
– – substantial recovery	3	1,500
– – – continuing significant disability	9	4,400
Loss of:		
– great toe	12	8,200
– both great toes	14	13,500
– one toe (other than great toe)	1	1,000
– two or more toes	9	4,400

Description of injury	*Level*	*Standard Amount £*
Partial loss of:		
– great toe	6	2,500
– both great toes	10	5,500

Appendix 2
GUIDE TO THE CRIMINAL INJURIES COMPENSATION SCHEME 2008

CONTENTS

SECTION 1 – INTRODUCTION

Purpose of this guide

1 This guide is for people who have applied, or are thinking of applying, for compensation under the Criminal Injuries Compensation Scheme 2008 (we call this 'the Scheme'). The 2008 Scheme applies to all applications received on or after 3 November 2008.
2 Other guides are available about previous Schemes. If you applied before 3 November 2008, and you want a copy of an earlier guide, please call our freephone number 0800 358 3601.
3 This guide tells you some of the main issues that are taken into account in deciding whether or not you can get an award.
4 Section 5 (page 35) explains what you can do if you are not happy with the decision you get.
5 You can get a copy of the Criminal Injuries Compensation Schemes on our website at www.cica.gov.uk. You can ask for a paper copy of the 2008 Scheme by writing to us at:

CICA
Tay House
300 Bath Street
Glasgow
G2 4LN

or calling our freephone number on 0800 358 3601.

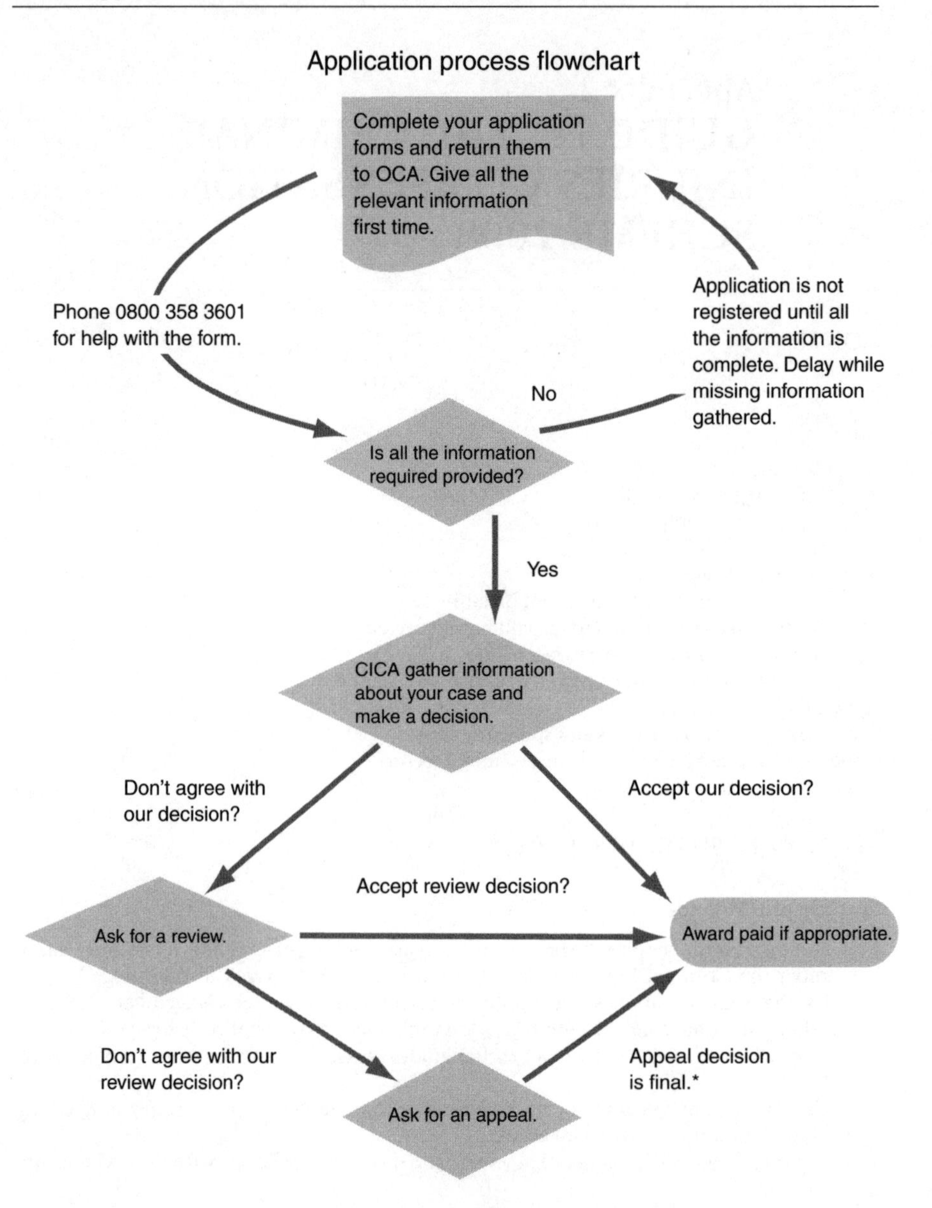

*The appeal decision is final, unless decided otherwise by Judicial Review.

What is the Criminal Injuries Compensation Scheme?

6 The Criminal Injuries Compensation Scheme (the Scheme) is a government funded scheme that allows blameless victims of violent crime to get a financial award. Under the Scheme, each type of injury is given a value. The values together form a list that we call 'the tariff'. The award can never fully compensate for all the injuries suffered, but is recognition of public sympathy for the blameless victim.

7 The minimum tariff payment is £1,000 and the maximum tariff payment for a single injury is £250,000. In certain circumstances you may also be entitled to additional payments for loss of earnings and special expenses (see Appendix 4 for more details). The maximum overall award is £500,000 – this is when we have added an award for injury to an award for loss of earnings or special expenses.

8 The Scheme is for people injured in England, Wales and Scotland ('Great Britain'). Northern Ireland has its own Scheme, as do many other countries. If you were injured outside Great Britain there is more information in Section 6.

9 The rules of the Scheme and the value of the awards paid are set by Parliament. CICA administers these rules.

What compensation is available?

10 We can consider claims for compensation for the following:

- Personal injury (including a single incident of abuse). (See Appendix 1 for more details.)
- Personal injury following a period of abuse. (See Appendix 2 for more details.)
- Fatal injuries, including financial dependency and loss of parental services. (See Appendix 3 for more details.)
- Loss of earnings and special expenses. (See Appendix 4 for more details.)

SECTION 2 – WHO CAN GET AN AWARD?

1 You may get an award if:

- **You were physically or mentally injured (or both) as a result of a crime of violence in Scotland, England or Wales.**
  - You do not need to be a British citizen to apply.
  - In assessing an injury we will take account of any relevant medical conditions you had before you were injured.
- **You were the dependent and/or a close relative of a person who died as the result of a violent crime.**
  - A close relative normally means the husband, wife, civil partner (or a person who was living in the same household as the victim in a relationship like a husband, wife or civil partner), parent or child.
- **You were injured in the last two years.** This time limit may be disregarded, but only in exceptional circumstances where:
  - the circumstances of your injury meant that we could not reasonably have expected you to apply within the two-year time limit; and
  - it is still possible to investigate your claim.
- **Your injuries are serious enough to qualify for the lowest (minimum) award we can pay under the Scheme.** The minimum award is £1,000. If your injury is not serious enough to qualify for a £1,000 payment we will not be able to make an award.
- **You were injured as a result of someone committing an offence of trespass on a railway.** To claim you must:

  - be a railway employee who has witnessed or been present when someone was killed or seriously injured as a result of the crime, or involved in its immediate aftermath (the events that happened straight after the incident); and
  - have suffered a physical injury or a disabling mental injury which can be medically verified (for more serious mental trauma we will need a psychiatric diagnosis).

2 You cannot get an award if:

- you were injured before 1 August 1964;
- you have already applied for compensation for the same criminal injury, whether under this or any other Scheme; (if you deliberately apply for compensation for the same injury more than once, you may be prosecuted for attempted fraud.); and/or
- the injury happened **before** 1 October 1979 and you and the person who injured you were living together at the time as members of the same family. This is because the Scheme changed at this time.

Making sure that the person who injured you cannot benefit from your claim

3 In general, the Scheme does not allow any person who causes an injury to benefit from an award paid to the victim. We will not pay an award if there is a continuing close link between you (the victim) and the offender and it is likely that the offender would benefit from your award.

Conviction of the person who injured you

4 You may be able to get an award even if the person who injured you is not prosecuted.

Violent crime

5 Although there is no legal definition of the term 'a crime of violence', we usually expect it to have involved a physical attack, although this is not always the case. Examples of attacks where you may be eligible to claim an award include:

- assault (physical or sexual);
- wounding;
- where you were injured as a direct result of a crime of arson;
- where there was a deliberate attempt to poison you;
- where an animal was deliberately set on you with the intent of causing you injury;
- where someone deliberately ran you down with a vehicle (this does not include where you were injured because of an accident).

Other times when a claim may be possible

6 There are very few other times when you may still be entitled to get an award under the Scheme even though you were not the victim of a crime of violence. These are:

- you were injured as a result of trespass on the railway (there are conditions to this criteria see page 8 above);
- you were injured while trying to help prevent a crime or helping a police officer catch a criminal. However, we will only make a payment if we are satisfied that you were taking an exceptional risk and that this risk was justified in all the circumstances.

Personal injury

7 For the purposes of the Scheme a personal injury is:

- physical injury (including a fatal injury);

- sexual abuse/assault;
- mental injury;
- mental or physical disease that is directly related to a crime of violence.

8 If you were not physically injured **we will not consider making an award for mental injury or disease alone**, unless:

- you were put in reasonable fear of immediate physical harm; or
- you witnessed or were present when someone, with whom you had a close relationship of love and affection (including someone you are not related to), was injured (including a fatal injury), or you were closely involved in the **immediate** aftermath (events that happened straight after the incident); or
- you were the non-consenting victim of a sexual offence; or
- you were a railway employee and you witnessed and were present when a person was injured (or killed) while they were trespassing on the railway, or you were involved in the **immediate** aftermath of such an incident.

Immediate aftermath

9 By 'aftermath' we mean events that happened straight after the incident. So although you did not witness or were not present during the incident in which a loved one was killed or injured you may be entitled to make a claim for mental injury if you were involved in the immediate aftermath. This also applies if you are employed by the railways and did not actually see the injury happening. When we say 'immediate' we are referring to the incident itself and not the events that might follow an incident (such as dealing with the police and medical authorities). To be considered for an award as a result of being involved in the immediate aftermath you must have arrived at the incident straight after it occurred and suffered a mental injury as a result. We would need confirmation from a medical practitioner that this was the case.

10 If you want more advice on whether or not you can make a claim, please call our freephone helpline number on **0800 358 3601**.

Conduct and character

11 The Scheme is intended to compensate **blameless** victims of crime. Before making an award we have to check that your behaviour did not contribute to the incident where you got your injuries. We also have to take account of your criminal record, if you have one. This may mean we refuse your claim, or offer you a reduced amount of compensation. These are some of the things we must take into account when deciding about your award:

12 Your behaviour before, during or after the incident where you were injured

13 We are likely to refuse or reduce your claim if:

- you willingly took part in a fight;
- you were acting in an aggressive or threatening way and provoked the incident where you were injured;
- there was a history of assaults or fighting between you and the person who injured you;
- you were injured as a result of challenging someone over a previous incident;
- you were taking part in illegal activities when you were injured;
- you did not take reasonable steps to get out of a situation where it was likely you would get hurt.

Excessive consumption of alcohol or use of illicit drugs

14 We take the excessive consumption of alcohol or the use of illicit drugs into account if we consider that their use contributed to the incident in which you were injured. This may result in us reducing or refusing your award.

Criminal record

15 The Scheme says we must reduce or refuse an award if you have a criminal record. In deciding how much of a reduction we will make, we will look at the length of any criminal record and the time that has passed since the last offence. However, we are likely to completely refuse an award, or make a very substantial reduction, if you have a conviction for a serious crime. See Appendix 5 for information on how we will normally decide what effect your criminal record will have on your award.

16 We will ignore any convictions which can be treated as spent under the Rehabilitation of Offenders Act 1974.

Failure to report the crime quickly

17 We expect you to report the crime immediately (to ensure the best chance of catching the person who injured you). Normally we will refuse a claim if you do not report the incident to the police straightaway. There are a few exceptions to this, for example:

- in certain cases of child abuse;
- if the kind of injuries you got meant we could not reasonably have expected you to make a full report to the police immediately.

18 We normally expect you to report the crime to the police. However, there may be circumstances where we accept that it was more reasonable for you to have reported it to another authority (for example, military police, a prison warden or the chief officer in an institution for people with mental illnesses).

Failure to co-operate with the police and courts

19 We expect you to have done everything possible to help the police catch and convict the person who injured you, including making a full statement to the police and cooperating in bringing the person who injured you to justice.

20 We appreciate that you may be reluctant to bring charges (for example, if you fear a revenge attack or reprisal). However, since the Scheme is publicly funded, it is important that you have done your public duty by reporting the crime and co-operating with the police.

Failure to co-operate with us

21 It is your responsibility to help us collect the information we need to investigate your claim. For example, we may refuse your claim if:

- you fail to give us the information we need in order to check something you have claimed for;
- you fail to attend a medical examination that lets us verify your injuries;
- you don't tell us about something that would affect your claim;
- you fail to tell us if you change your contact details. If you tell us about a change of address, please make sure you get confirmation from us that we have changed your records. Otherwise we may lose contact, which means we will withhold your claim.

Other matters

22 The Scheme is funded by the taxpayer, so we need to be certain that anyone applying has not deliberately avoided paying their taxes or deliberately claimed state benefits they were not entitled to. If we discover someone has been earning money which they have not been declaring for tax purposes or fraudulently claiming state benefits, we are likely to take this into account when considering your application.

23 **When we make an award because someone has died as a result of a crime of violence, we need to take account of the conduct and character of both the applicant and the deceased.**

SECTION 3 – APPLYING FOR COMPENSATION

1 **You do not need a paid representative (for example a solicitor or a claims management company) to apply for criminal injuries compensation. If you choose paid representation we cannot meet the cost of this and you will have to pay these costs yourself.**

2 You can get free advice and help with completing your application form from us on **0800 358 3601**.

3 Victim Support is the independent national charity for people affected by crime. Victim Support gives free and confidential support and practical help to victims and witnesses of crime and this can include helping you with your application. You can contact them by:

- phoning the Victim Supportline on **0845 30 30 900** (England and Wales) or **0845 60 39 213** (Scotland);
- visiting their website at **www.victimsupport.org**; or
- emailing **supportline@victimsupport.org.uk**

4 Victim Support cannot provide legal advice.

5 You can also get advice from your local Citizens Advice service or a law centre, or from a welfare rights organisation. If you belong to a trade union, they may be able to help.

6 You can get a friend or a relative to complete your application form on your behalf and/or represent you.

What happens if you are trying to make other claims about the same incident?

7 The Scheme pays awards taking into account other payments for the same injury. We may not start to process your claim until you have confirmed that you are not claiming from anyone else because of the same incident. To avoid your claim being 'out of time' you should still apply to us within two years of the incident. We may hold your case from the date of application, to allow you the time to pursue other parties. We will not normally work on your case while it is being held.

8 If we decide to hold your case, let us know immediately when any other claim is settled. You must let us know what payments you have got from other sources as we will need to take these off any award you may be due from us.

How do you apply for an award?

9 We have application forms which deal with different types of injuries and circumstances. To ensure you complete the correct forms you can either:

- go to our website at **www.cica.gov.uk**; or
- contact our telephone support team on **0800 358 3601**.

10 You will get help to choose the right forms and our team will be able to give you advice on whether you are likely to qualify ('eligibility') and help completing the application form. They can also help if you have difficulty reading or writing.

Main types of form

Compensation for personal injury after a single incident

11 Complete this form if:

- You were injured because of a single incident.
- You are applying on behalf of someone else who has suffered a personal injury as a result of a single incident (in which case you should answer the questions on the form as if you were the person who was injured).

Compensation for personal injury after a period of abuse

12 Complete this form if:

- You have suffered a physical, sexual or mental injury (or both) because you were abused over a period of time.
- You are applying on behalf of someone who has been injured as a result of being abused over a period of time (answer the questions as though you were the person who was injured).

Compensation for a fatal injury

13 Complete this form if:

- Your parent, child, husband, wife or partner has died because of a crime of violence.
- You are claiming on behalf of a child or an adult who is deemed incapable of managing their own affairs whose parent, child, husband, wife or partner has died as a result of a crime of violence.

14 This form also lets you make a claim for personal injury if you:

- were physically injured in the same incident; or
- suffered a disabling mental injury as a result of witnessing and being present during the incident, or its immediate aftermath (see Section 2, pages 7-8 for more details on eligibility).

Other forms

15 There are a number of reasons why you may need to complete a further application form, as well as one of the three main ones mentioned above.

Applying on behalf of someone you have parental responsibility for

16 Fill in one of the main application forms (single incident, abuse or fatal injury) answering the questions on behalf of the child or young person.
17 If the child is under 12 years of age you should sign the form on their behalf. If the young person is over 12 years of age, both of you will need to sign the form.
18 You will then need to complete a short extra form giving us your details and evidence that you have parental rights. This evidence will need to be a full original birth certificate unless the child is in care and you are the representative of a local authority.
19 If the child is in care, we expect the local authority to apply for compensation if they have parental responsibility. The application (and any later applications for review or appeal) should be signed by someone who is authorised to do so, on behalf of the local authority, and a copy of the care order should be provided.
20 If no-one is legally entitled to act for the child, you should get help from the Official Solicitor (the person who acts on behalf of those who cannot represent themselves) to apply in England and Wales. If you are in Scotland, a tutor or guardian may need to be appointed. We cannot make these arrangements for you. Wherever possible, try to complete all necessary formalities on the child's behalf before applying, to avoid delays later on. If the incident you are claiming for happened some time ago, please send us the application as quickly as possible.
21 If you are not sure who is responsible for the child, you can get advice, for example, from your local Citizens Advice service.
22 We pay awards to people under 18 directly into an interest-earning bank account. The money is not paid out until the applicant becomes an adult and is able to manage the funds for themselves (see Section 4 on payment arrangements).

Applying on behalf of an adult who lacks capacity to conduct proceedings or is legally defined as incapable of managing his or her own affairs

23 Fill in one of the main application forms (single incident, abuse or fatal injury) answering the questions on behalf of the person you are representing. Sign the form on their behalf.

24 You will then need to complete an additional one-sheet application form giving us your details. In all cases where an adult lacks capacity we will need full details about your status and the extent of your powers as well as evidence that you are entitled to act on their behalf.

25 If the person does not have someone acting on their behalf that is entitled to do so, then you could consider applying to the Court of Protection for the appointment of a deputy (England and Wales) or a financial welfare guardian or for an intervention order (Scotland). There is more information at **www.publicguardian.gov.uk/** (England and Wales) or **www.publicguardianscotland.gov.uk/** (Scotland). This will allow you to:

- authorise all our enquiries;
- decide whether to accept an award;
- ask for a review; or
- appeal to the Tribunals Service – Criminal Injuries Compensation.

26 In these circumstances, we will also need you to give us medical evidence that the person you are representing lacks capacity or is 'incapable by reason of mental disorder', within the meanings of the Mental Capacity Act 2005 (England and Wales) or Adults with Incapacity (Scotland) Act 2000.

27 If a person lacks capacity or is not capable of managing their own affairs, it is likely that their award will be put into a trust or paid to the deputy appointed by the Court of Protection or a financial welfare guardian in Scotland. We will pay the costs of setting up the trust as a 'special expense', when this is approved by a claims officer, within the overall £500,000 limit (including the tariff injury award).

Using a representative

28 If you want a representative (paid or free) to deal with your claim on your behalf you will need to complete a further, single-sheet application form. On this, you can tell us who you want to represent you and how we can contact them. By signing this form you are confirming that you are responsible for paying any fee. The CICA will not pay the cost of any representation.

Applying for loss of earnings and special expenses if you expect to be unable to work for more than 28 weeks

29 Appendix 4 gives further information about who is eligible for loss of earnings and special expenses and explains how we work these out.

30 You do not need to apply for loss of earnings at the same time as you make your personal injury claim, but you do need to make your claim before your personal injury claim is finalised. If you think you will be eligible for loss of earnings and/or special expenses, you should complete the short supplementary form called, 'Unable to work for more than 28 weeks'. If, after our initial assessment, we decide you are eligible for a tariff payment, we will ask you for the full details of your claim for loss of earnings. At this time we will ask you to provide us with the necessary supporting information.

Loss of earnings

31 If you are claiming loss of earnings, you will need to give us evidence to show what you have lost. When we get your application form we will write to you to tell you what evidence we will need. For example:

- three months' payslips for the period immediately before the injury; or
- a copy of your P60; or
- a firm job offer showing your salary; or
- evidence from HM Revenue and Customs of your declared earnings; or
- if you are self employed a copy of your tax return; or

- a certified copy of your accounts for the three years immediately preceding the incident.

32 If you were not employed at the time of the incident and you expect to lose future earnings as a result of the injury, the kind of evidence we may need will include:

- evidence that you were in full-time education; or
- evidence that you were on a training course which was likely to lead to full-time employment; or
- evidence of past earnings.

33 In all cases, we will need medical evidence to support your claim for loss of earnings.

Special expenses

34 You may be able to get extra compensation to cover special expenses if your injury prevents you from working for more than 28 weeks, or, if you are not normally employed, you are incapacitated to a similar extent. This can be done using the same application form as for loss of earnings. There is more information about special expenses in Appendix 4.

Your consent and signature

35 When you sign the application form, you are giving us your consent for the release of all the records, evidence and other information about you and the circumstances of your injury which will help us make the right decision about your application. This will include:

- information about your medical condition;
- the evidence you gave the police; and
- a criminal records check.

36 It may also include (if you are claiming for lost earnings or special expenses) information about your income, tax and benefits situation.

37 You are also confirming that the information you provide on the application is true. If we find that you have deliberately given us false information or have failed to give us information we have asked for (for example, criminal records or details of other claims) we may refuse your application. We may also refuse your application if you make another claim for the same injury without writing on the new application form that it is a duplicate of a previous application.

How will we deal with your application?

38 When we have a fully completed application from you, we will give you a personal reference number which will help us to identify it quickly if you need to contact us. By the end of 2009 you will also be able to apply online. When this happens, we will send you a copy of the completed form in order that you can check the content and add your signature. We will need you to return the signed version of the form before we can register your case.

39 The first thing we do when we get your form is to list the evidence we will need to collect in order to assess your claim (we call this our 'case strategy'). The evidence we normally need includes:

- confirmation from the police that a crime of violence was committed and that you were a blameless victim (we will also need to collect witness statements to confirm your role in the incident which led to your injury);
- a check on criminal convictions. We will compare the information from the police with the information you put on your application form. If you have convictions you haven't told us about, we may refuse your claim;

- where appropriate, a report from your doctor confirming what injuries you received and giving us an estimate of how long it will take you to recover.
- depending on the seriousness of the injuries we may need additional reports from specialists. We may also need to check that you did not already have any conditions that might have an affect on your claim (we refer to these as 'pre-existing conditions'); and
- if you want to claim loss of earnings or special expenses (if your injury prevents you from working for more than 28 weeks, or, if you are not normally employed, you are incapacitated to a similar extent) you will need to give us evidence to support your claim. This is likely to include information about your earnings before and after the incident, details of tax and national insurance contributions and income from benefits.

40 One of our regional casework teams will handle your claim. If you phone for advice or an update on your claim, you will speak to one of our telephone support advisers. We will always try to answer your query while you are on the line but if we can't do this, we will arrange to get in touch with you at a convenient time.

41 The length of time needed to assess your claim will vary depending on how complicated it is. For example, claims involving loss of earnings and special expenses will take longer than those involving only a tariff payment. You will be responsible for giving us any evidence we ask you for. There is more information about how long it takes on average to resolve cases on our website or you can speak to our telephone support staff.

42 When we have all the evidence we need to decide your case, it will be passed to a claims officer. Claims officers decide cases on what is called 'the balance of probabilities'. This means that their decision is based on what is more likely to have happened than not have happened. We do not need to have something proved 'beyond a reasonable doubt'. As soon as possible after the decision has been made, we will write to tell you, or your representative, what it is. If we have reduced or refused an award, we will tell you why. We will send you information about what to do if you don't agree with our decision.

43 If you decide to accept our award, you or your representative must complete and return the acceptance form within 90 days of it being sent to the contact address we have on your file. If you do not get an acceptance back within 90 days, and you have not asked for a review in writing, then we may withdraw the award.

44 If you disagree with our decision, you can ask for it to be reviewed by another claims officer. We send you a review form when we issue the original decision. Section 5 of this guide tells you how to request a review. It also tells you how to make an appeal to the Tribunals Service – Criminal Injuries Compensation which is independent of the Authority. You can make an appeal if you remain unhappy after a review decision.

45 We sometimes need to make special arrangements for paying an award, to take account of the circumstances of the victim or other relevant issues. Section 4 of this guide provides more information on payment arrangements.

SECTION 4 – PAYMENT OF AWARDS

1 The Scheme says we can make certain arrangements about the payment or repayment of awards. In deciding about this, we take the applicant's interests into account, as well as considering public policy.

2 Wherever possible, we settle applications by offering a single payment of compensation – what we call a final award. But we can only do this if your medical condition and financial losses are clear. If there is likely to be a long delay in getting this information, but it is clear that you are eligible for compensation, we may make one or more interim payments.

3 The Scheme allows us to agree with an applicant that the award can be used to buy an annuity to give the applicant an income over a period of years, instead of a single lump sum payment. If this is something you think would be appropriate in your case, you will need to tell us when you get an offer of an award.

Payment of award to adults who manage their own financial affairs

4 At the moment we pay our awards by cheque to the applicant or their nominated representative. However to protect against fraud, by 2011 we will aim to have most payments made electronically, in the name of the applicant. We will not accept an instruction to make your award payable to anyone else. If you have agreed to pay someone to represent you, then it is your responsibility to pay them their fee once you get your award.

5 We will make separate arrangements for people who don't have bank accounts.

Payment of awards to adults who do not manage their own financial affairs

6 Where an adult is legally defined as not capable of managing their own affairs we will normally pay their award to the person who has legal authority to manage their finances. We will need confirmation of the representative's status at the start of the application process.

Payments of awards to children and young people

7 If an applicant is under 18 when they accept an award, it is our general policy to put the award in an interest-earning deposit account in their name. The award will be paid to the applicant (together with all interest earned) when they are 18.

8 We will allow advances on the award if these are needed for the sole benefit, education or welfare of the child or young person. If we make an advance payment, we will need evidence – normally a receipt – proving that it has been used for the purposes intended. If we don't get this evidence, we will not allow any further advances. We may allow for the payment of the full award to a young person who is 16 or 17 years of age and living independently.

9 We give full guidance about how we manage awards for young people when we make our award offer.

When is an award final?

Re-consideration of a case

10 Up until the point we make a final payment, we may reconsider our decision and take account of new evidence or a change of circumstances. If we are reconsidering your award we will write to you to tell you what we are doing and why. We will invite you to give us your views on what we are reconsidering.

Re-opening a case

11 Once you have accepted a final award and received your payment, your case will not be re-opened except in rare circumstances. We will only re-open a case if there has been such a change in your medical condition that an injustice would occur if the case were not re-opened, or in cases where a person has since died as a result of their injuries.

12 We will not normally re-open a case unless it is within two years of the final decision. If you ask us to re-open on medical grounds a case that has been closed for more than two years, you will have to give us enough evidence to support the case for re-opening.

Fraud and repayment of awards

13 If we get information that leads us to believe that you gave us false information about your application, we may refer the matter to the police for investigation.

14 If we decide that you did give us, or the police, false information, we will take steps to recover the award. We may also seek to recover the award if we find that you are living with the person who inflicted the injuries for which you claimed.

SECTION 5 – REVIEWS AND APPEALS

Asking for a decision to be reviewed

1 If you disagree with the original decision and want us to review it, you need to send us your written application for a review within 90 days of the date of the original decision. You'll need to enclose any additional evidence that you wish us to consider in support of your claim.

2 Our decision letter will tell you what evidence we considered in order to reach our original decision.

3 We will not accept any new evidence after the 90 days unless we have given you an extension. We will do this if it was not reasonable to have expected you to have made the request within the time limit. If this is the case, you will need to write to us. You can ask for an extension even after the 90 days have passed but we will only grant this if there are exceptional circumstances.

4 When we get your request for a review along with all your supporting information, a claims officer, other than the one who made the original decision, will look at the whole application again. The review decision can be more or less favourable than the original decision, or the original decision may be unchanged. It is important that you understand that while a possible outcome of a review is that you might get a bigger award, it is also possible that you will get a lower award or no award at all.

Appealing to the Tribunals Service – Criminal Injuries Compensation (Tribunal)

5 If you disagree with a review decision you can appeal to the Tribunal in accordance with Tribunal Procedure Rules. You can find these rules on the Tribunal website at **www.cicap.gov.uk/RulesLegislation/rulesLegislation.htm** or by writing to the Tribunal at the address below.

6 When we send you our review decision, we will send you the form to use to ask for an appeal. You will need to fill in the form, including reasons why you are appealing and any extra material, and send it to the Tribunal (not to us) so that they get it within 90 days of the date of the review decision. You can ask the Tribunal to extend this period, but you must do so within the 90 days. The Tribunal's address is:

Tribunals Service – Criminal Injuries Compensation
Wellington House
134-136 Wellington Street
Glasgow
G2 2XL

7 The Tribunal will explain its procedures when it gets your request for an appeal. If your appeal proceeds to an oral hearing, it is likely that a representative from CICA will be at the hearing in order to explain our decision. The members and staff of the Tribunal are entirely independent of us and consider the whole application again. They may make a decision that is more favourable or less favourable than the review decision, or the review decision can stay the same. The Tribunal decision is final, unless decided otherwise by Judicial Review.

SECTION 6 – IF YOU WERE INJURED OUTSIDE GREAT BRITAIN

1 If you were injured outside Great Britain, you may be able to claim under a similar Scheme operated by the country concerned. If you were injured in a country outside of the EU please contact the Foreign and Commonwealth Office.

2 If you are a UK resident and were injured in another EU country, we can help you apply for compensation from that country. Please call our EU Assistance Team on **0800 358 3601** or email **eucat@cica.gsi.gov.uk**. Details of compensation schemes in other countries can be found on the EU Judicial Atlas on the internet.

3 If you were injured in Northern Ireland, you should contact:

The Compensation Agency
Royston House
34 Upper Queen Street
Belfast
BT1 6FD
Phone: 02890 249 944

SECTION 7 – HOW TO TELL US ABOUT THE SERVICE YOU HAVE RECEIVED

Our standards of service

1 You can expect us to deal with your application politely and confidentially. We are trying to improve the time it takes us to deal with applications but due to the volume of claims, and the time needed to confirm the facts of a case, it is usually many months (and sometimes more than a year) before we can settle your case. Sometimes it is in the applicant's best interests that we do not settle the claim until the full extent of the injuries are known – and this might be much longer than a year.
2 We are constantly striving to improve our service standards. For information on our current service standards and our average processing times please see our website **www.cica.gov.uk** or ask our telephone support team on **0800 358 3601**.
3 We offer a full telephone support service from 8.30am to 8.00pm (Monday to Friday) and 9.00am to 1.00pm on a Saturday.
4 To give us feedback about excellent service, or to make a complaint, please contact the CICA Customer Liaison Team on **0800 358 3601**.

Or email: **customer.feedback@cica.gsi.gov.uk**

Or write to:

Customer Liaison Team
Criminal Injuries Compensation Authority
Tay House
300 Bath Street
Glasgow
G2 4LN

5 Please quote your case reference number when you contact us.
6 We have a formal procedure for dealing with complaints, treating each one individually. We aim to resolve any issues as quickly as possible.

Stage 1: Regional area

7 All complaints are dealt with initially by the regional team managing your claim. They will respond to you within 21 days.

Stage 2: Customer liaison team

8 If you are not satisfied with our first response, our customer liaison team will independently investigate and reply to you within 21 days.

Stage 3: Senior manager

9 If you remain dissatisfied, a senior member of our corporate service management team will investigate and respond to your complaint within 21 days. Our Board of Directors

(including the Chief Executive) will be made aware through monthly reporting about all complaints that reach this stage.

10 After you have exhausted the stages above, if you are still not happy with how we dealt with your complaint, you can take the matter further.

11 You can complain through your Member of Parliament to the Parliamentary and Health Service Ombudsman (if you are in England and Wales). In Scotland, you can complain directly to the Scottish Public Services Ombudsman (SPSO). In both cases, they will need to be certain that you have exhausted CICA's complaints process. The Ombudsman carries out independent investigations into complaints about unfair or improper actions or poor service by UK government departments and their agencies. You can get more details from:

England and Wales

The Parliamentary and Health Service Ombudsman
Millbank Tower
Millbank
London
SW1P 4QP
Phone: **0345 015 4033**
Email: **phso.enquiries@ombudsman.org.uk**
Fax: **0300 061 4000**
Website: **www.ombudsman.org.uk**

Scotland

12 Complaints to the Scottish Public Services Ombudsman must be sent in writing to:

SPSO
Freepost EH641
Edinburgh
EH3 0BR
Phone: **0800 377 7330**
Email: **ask@spso.org.uk**
Fax: **0800 377 7331**
Text: **0790 049 4372**
Website: **www.spso.org.uk**

APPENDIX 1 – CLAIMING FOR A PERSONAL INJURY

The tariff award

1 The tariff (pages 69-111) sets out what awards we can pay (before any deductions are made) if you have suffered a criminal injury. The tariff is available on our website or we can send a paper copy on request. The tariff is in two parts. The first is a list of 25 levels of compensation, ranging from level 1 (£1,000) to level 25 (£250,000).

2 The second part is a list of more than 400 injury descriptions, together with a level of compensation and amount of money we can pay for each. In most cases this is self-explanatory – you can find the description of the injury which you have suffered and check the amount of compensation which you can expect to receive (depending on rules regarding eligibility, reductions and so on).

3 It is worth noting that the tariff begins with those injuries which do not relate to a specific single part of the body, such as fatal injuries, multiple burns, mental illness, nerve damage and physical and sexual assault and abuse. It then uses a 'head to toe' approach, dealing first with injuries to the head and neck, followed by injuries to the arms, torso and legs.

4 The tariff cannot describe every possible injury. In the unlikely event that we receive an application for an injury which is not covered by the tariff, we will consult the Tribunals Service – Criminal Injuries Compensation about what might be the right level of compensation for the injury and then recommend to the Secretary of State that the injury and level of compensation are added to the tariff. In the meantime, we may make a provisional payment of up to 50 per cent of the value of the compensation payment which we recommend to the Secretary of State.

5 If your injury speeds up the onset of symptoms or makes worse a medical condition that you already had, the award we can make will be based only on the extent to which the medical condition was speeded up or made worse.

6 We will use the information we get from the hospital where you were treated, or from your doctor, to decide which tariff award, if any, is appropriate to your injuries. Although we may reduce or refuse your award because of your conduct or character, we cannot change the maximum amounts available for a particular type of injury because they are set by Parliament.

What happens when you have more than one injury?

Minor multiple injuries

7 This is the Scheme term for the minimum level of injuries we will pay compensation for. It covers cases where you did not get one single injury that is serious enough for a £1,000 minimum award, but you did have several less serious injuries like cuts, severe bruising, a black eye or hair pulled from the scalp. The term 'minor multiple injuries' does not mean that these injuries will seem minor to the person who suffered them.

8 We may make you an award for multiple minor injuries if you:

- suffered at least three injuries of this type; and
- if at least one of them was still troubling you significantly six weeks after the incident; and
- if the injuries meant that you had to visit your doctor at least twice in that six-week period.

Two or more serious injuries

9 If you had two or more injuries so serious that each on its own would qualify for compensation, we will pay you:

- 100 per cent of the full tariff value of the most serious injury;
- 30 per cent of the value of the next most serious injury;
- 15 per cent of the value of the third most serious injury.

10 The Scheme does not allow us to pay for more than three injuries.

APPENDIX 2 – CLAIMING AFTER A PERIOD OF ABUSE

1 If you, or someone for whom you have responsibility, has been injured because of a period of physical or sexual abuse, you can submit a claim for compensation.

Cases involving members of the same household or family

2 There are restrictions on making awards to people who were living as members of the same family in the same household as the person who injured them. Please see Section 2 for more details.

Reporting to the police

3 If you were abused as a child, we appreciate that you may not have felt able to report the

incident for some time after the abuse happened. No matter how long ago the abuse took place, you should report it to the police before you contact us about making a claim for compensation. We need to check with the police that the crime has been reported as this is our main protection against fraud. If you report the incident it may also help prevent more offences against other people. If you have not reported the incident to the police, and have no good reason for not doing so, it is likely that we will reject your application for compensation.

Time limits

4 Under the Scheme we expect you to send us your application within two years of the date of the incident. We will only consider applications outside this time limit where:

- the circumstances of your injury meant that we could not reasonably have expected you to apply within the two-year time limit; and
- it is still possible to investigate your claim.

5 These special circumstances may apply to a person who was sexually abused as a child but who could not report the abuse until they became an adult. However, we would expect that the person reports the abuse as soon as it is reasonable for them to do so.

Applications on behalf of children

6 Under the Scheme, an application on behalf of a child (under the age of 18) must be made by an adult with parental responsibility for the child. Usually this person is one of the child's parents. But if the child has been abused within the immediate family, this may be impossible. Please see Section 3 for more details about making an application on behalf of a child.

Further enquiries

7 Before we can make an award, we have to know:

- the full circumstances of the incident and the injury;
- how serious the injury was; and
- how well you are recovering from the injury.

8 We may get this information from the police, hospitals, doctors and anyone else listed on the application form. You can help us by sending any other supporting information with the application itself, such as medical or psychological reports that you already hold. Please note that we may not pay for medical reports that you have arranged.

APPENDIX 3 – FATAL INJURIES

Who can we compensate when there has been a fatal injury?

1 To get compensation you must be what the Scheme calls a 'qualifying claimant'. This is someone who, when the victim died, was in one of the following groups:

- The victim's wife, husband or partner registered under the Civil Partnerships Act 2004. The couple must have either been living together immediately before the victim died, or, if they were not living together, this must have been because of infirmity or ill health.
- The victim's former wife, husband or partner registered under the Civil Partnerships Act 2004, but only if the victim was supporting them financially immediately before the date the victim died.
- The unmarried partner of the victim, if they were living together as husband and

wife or as partners of the same sex (although not registered under the Civil Partnerships Act 2004), immediately before the victim died and for at least two years before that.

- The natural parents of the victim, or the person or people the victim treated as their own parents.
- The children of the victim, or the people who the victim accepted as their children or who were dependent on the victim.

2 The definition of 'child' is not limited to a person below the age of 18. It includes adult children and an unborn child of the person who has died, conceived before they died and born alive after they died. The parents of a victim can receive compensation whatever the age of the victim.

3 You may be able to get compensation if the victim has died from their injuries, even if we paid compensation to the victim before they died.

4 A person who was responsible for the death of a victim cannot get compensation as a result of the death.

5 We cannot pay compensation to a former husband, wife or registered same-sex partner or someone who was otherwise estranged from the victim immediately before the date they died.

Funeral expenses

6 Whoever paid for the funeral (whether or not they are eligible for other compensation) can apply for these expenses to be paid back. Even if you have a criminal record, we will still be able to refund you for reasonable funeral expenses following the victim's death. But if the victim had a criminal record, we have to take this into account even when we consider an application for funeral expenses.

7 If you are applying for the cost of a funeral, you will need to send us the receipts and evidence that you paid them. There will be limits on what we consider to be a reasonable cost.

General rules for compensation

8 As with all claims, we must consider the victim's (deceased's) behaviour during the incident and their character (particularly their criminal record) when deciding whether we should offer compensation, reduced compensation, or no compensation at all. In the case of fatal applications we have to apply these rules to the victim and to the applicant.

9 We must take account of the applicant's criminal record when deciding an application for compensation. We look only at convictions which are not 'spent' under the Rehabilitation of Offenders Act. This means that when the victim has died, we have to take account of any 'unspent' criminal convictions which either they or the applicant had.

Types of compensation for death as a result of a criminal injury

10 If you qualify for compensation and the victim died as a result of a criminal injury, you may be able to get an award made up of one or more of these compensation payments:

- The 'standard amount' of compensation;
- Dependency;
- Loss of parental services, if you are a child aged under 18.

Standard amount

11 The standard amount of compensation recognises the fact that someone very close to you has died as a result of a crime of violence. No amount of money can make up for the death of a close relative – the standard amount is a gesture of public sympathy for the grief caused by the death.

12 If there is only one qualifying claimant, the standard amount of compensation is £11,000. If there is more than one qualifying claimant, the standard amount of compensation is £5,500 for each person.

13 It is important to remember that we have no choice about how much compensation we can pay in these cases. The amounts of £5,500 and £11,000 are set out in the 'tariff of injuries' in the Scheme.

Dependency

14 If you are a qualifying claimant and the death of your loved one has led to financial loss, or if you were dependent on them for care, you may qualify for extra compensation. This may be the case if, for example, they looked after the family and their death means that you have to change from full-time to part-time employment. The period of loss for which we may be able to provide compensation starts from the date the victim died.

15 To work out the compensation for loss of financial support, we take account of the household income as it was before the victim's death and compare it with the income after their death. We work it out up until the qualifying claimant would have become financially independent of the victim. In the case of a husband, wife or partner, this period will usually run until the victim would have retired. In the case of children, this period will usually run until they finish their full-time education. We will use a process similar to that for working out future loss of earnings, involving a multiplicand and a multiplier, to produce a lump sum (see Appendix 4 for more details).

Loss of parental services

16 A qualifying claimant aged under 18 at the date the victim died may be able to get compensation on top of any amount for dependency for what is called 'loss of parental services'. This is an amount of money to provide some small recognition of the tasks parents carry out for their children. The current compensation level for loss of parental services is the equivalent of £2,000 for every year until the child reaches 18. We will apply a multiplier to produce a lump sum (see Appendix 4 for more details).

Personal Injury

17 If you sustained a personal injury (either physical or mental) at the time of the victim's death, you may be entitled to an additional award of compensation. If you sustained a mental injury, it is important that you meet the criteria set out in the Scheme. This means you either witnessed and were present when the person with whom you had a close relationship of love and affection died, or you were closely involved in the immediate aftermath.

18 If you apply for this additional personal injury compensation, we will give you two case reference numbers. This is because we need to treat these as two separate cases.

Award to a victim before they die

19 We may be able to award compensation after a victim's death even if they got an award for their injury before they died. If the victim has died because of their injury, qualifying claimants may receive the 'standard amount' of compensation whether or not we compensated the victim while they were still alive. We can also pay reasonable funeral expenses.

20 We may also be able to pay for the family's loss as a result of financial dependency. If we compensated the victim before they died for their loss of earnings, we would have to reduce any compensation to their family under this heading, to avoid a double payment.

21 If you apply for compensation where the victim had already had compensation before they died and it is more than two years since we settled their case, we can only deal with your application if it will not need extensive enquiries. This means there would need to be little doubt that their death was directly caused by the criminal injury.

Death following, but not caused by, a criminal injury

22 If the victim's death was due to some cause other than their criminal injury, we cannot compensate anyone else for their death, or make any awards for loss of parental services. But if we could have compensated the victim for their loss of earnings or for special expenses (for example, the cost of their medical care) and the victim dies before the claim is finalised we may be able to pay this after their death to a qualifying claimant who was financially dependent on them.

23 The rules on dependency apply similarly to how they would if the injury had caused the victim's death. The rules about compensating victims for loss of earnings will also apply (see Appendix 4).

24 If you are applying for compensation under this heading, you will need to fill in a supplementary application form for this.

APPENDIX 4 – LOSS OF EARNINGS AND SPECIAL EXPENSES

1 As well as your tariff payment, we can compensate you if you can show that:

- you have lost earnings, or lost the capacity to earn your living, as a direct result of the injury which we have agreed to compensate you for; and
- your loss lasted longer than 28 full weeks. The period of 28 weeks will usually run from the date of the injury. But if you were off work for several separate periods for the same injury which add up to more than 28 weeks, you would also be able to claim for loss of earnings or earning capacity.

2 You cannot get loss of earnings for the first 28 weeks of loss.

Eligibility for loss of earnings

3 You are only eligible to claim loss of earnings if your inability to work is as a direct result of a criminal injury for which we have agreed a tariff payment, and not entirely or partly from other things, such as:

- health problems before the injury, including mental health issues;
- health problems which arose after the injury but which were not caused by the incident;
- a previous injury or illness (caused perhaps by sport or an accident at work);
- the financial insecurity of your type of work; or
- you are self-employed, or have trading or cash-flow problems not connected with the injury.

4 You may be eligible for a payment towards:

- what you have already lost (past loss of earnings); and
- what you may lose as a result of not being able to return to work (future loss of earnings).

5 If we find you have been earning money without paying taxes or dishonestly receiving state benefits, we are likely to take this into account when considering your application.

6 If we have given you any interim payments we will ask for these back.

7 The Scheme sets an upper limit on the weekly (or yearly) amount of loss of earnings we can compensate for. This upper limit is one and a half times median gross weekly earnings at the time when we assess your claim. The Annual Survey of Hours and Earnings (ASHE) gives the current level and is available at **www.statistics.gov.uk/statBase/product.asp?vlnk=13101**

Past loss of earnings

8 Because we cannot pay compensation for loss of earnings or earning capacity for the first 28 weeks, we start the calculation of your loss of earnings at week 29 of your loss and this runs to:

- the date when you returned to work; or
- the date when you were fit to return to work; or
- whatever other date is reasonable in the circumstances of your case.

9 You will be expected to provide evidence supporting your claim for loss of earnings. This might be pay slips or a P60 for the period immediately before you were injured, or an offer of a job which you were unable to take up because you were injured. If you are self-employed, we will ask for a copy of your annual accounts. When we get your claim we will tell you what information we need from you and we will verify this as needed.

10 When we assess your past loss we have to take account of any financial benefits you get or are entitled to get either from your employer or through the benefit system. To claim past loss of earnings you need to be able to provide proof of:

- what you were earning, or could have been earning, before the incident;
- your income since the incident (including any payments from employers and benefits); and
- what you have lost because of your injury.

Future loss of earnings

11 We need to judge both what your income will be in the future and what it would have been if you had not been injured. We need to take account of:

- how long in the future you will be unable to work;
- what the effect of your injury will be on your long-term ability to earn;
- your work history and whether or not it was likely that you would have had future earnings;
- what your life expectancy is likely to be; and
- whether your injury means that you will receive a different level of pension than you would have received otherwise.

12 In general, we pay compensation as a single lump sum. So we need to find a single amount of money which represents the value of earnings or pension payments which might have stretched many years into the future.

13 We do not just compare your earnings before and after your injury. We have to look at your total income, including the sick pay you get from your employer, social security benefits, ill-health/injury pension and income from any other employment. We also take account of benefits you are entitled to. The Scheme says that if you could get any social security or other state benefits, we may delay making an award until you have taken steps to claim them.

14 We also have to reduce any award we make for your lost earnings if you have received payment for this from an insurance policy which someone else (such as your employer) paid for or contributed to. If you get payment for lost earnings from an insurance policy which you paid for yourself, we do not reduce your award.

15 To calculate what you will get, we take account of:

- what your future earnings would have been without the injury;
- what you can earn now;
- what you should be able to earn in the future; and
- what you should be able to get in benefits.

16 There are two different types of issue we have to look at when we make these calculations:

- how much money you will lose every year; and
- how long your loss will last for.

17 The first step is to work out how much you will lose each year. This figure is known as the 'multiplicand' and is the rate of loss at the date we assess your claim.

18 We begin by looking at what you earned before your injury and adjusting it, as far as

possible, to get a figure for what you would have been earning now (at the date we decide your claim) if you had not had the injury. For example, if average earnings in your industry have risen by 10 per cent since you had to stop working, we would add 10 per cent to the figure you used to earn. We will also take account of, for example, any firm offer of promotion you had before you were injured. We will consider making payments if the injury meant that you lost some or all of your right to an occupational pension. We will need clear evidence from you about all of these things.

19 We also have to consider any payments you may receive instead of your earnings (such as a pension or state benefits), and what is likely to happen to your income in the future. For this, we will need information from you, the Department for Work and Pensions, your employer or former employer, and any other organisation relevant to your claim. We will ask you for the information we need. However, any information you can give us about your pattern and history of work will help us decide your case more quickly.

20 We also have to assess your ability to work in the future. So, we must take your estimated future income (including benefits and earnings) from your loss of earnings claim. This is the case whether or not you are in a job at the time we decide your claim. One result of this is that your amount of loss may vary from year to year. This means that there may be different multiplicands for different periods of future loss. For example, you may be unable to work now but the information from your doctor may suggest that you will be able to start part-time work in two years' time, and able to take up full-time work in three years' time, but at a lower pay than you were earning before your injury. The multiplicand – the amount you are losing every year – will reduce as your earnings increase.

21 Generally, the compensation we pay is a single lump sum, so we need to convert your annual future loss (the multiplicand) into a single lump sum which we can pay now. The figure which makes this conversion is called the multiplier.

22 The size of the multiplier depends on how long you will be losing money – the longer your period of loss, the higher the multiplier. But it is not as simple as adding 'one' to the multiplier for each extra year of loss. This is because the award we pay is, in effect, the value now of your financial loss into the future. Normally you would have received it year by year. Since we pay the award as a single lump sum, we have to take account of the interest you could gain from investing it as soon as you receive it. Another way of looking at it is that, as you will get your money early, we have to make a discount for early payment. It is the multiplier which 'translates' your yearly loss figure into a single lump sum.

23 More information on loss of earnings and special expenses is available from our telephone support team on **0800 358 3601**.

Special expenses

24 The Scheme allows us to consider claims for practical, medical and care costs, called 'special expenses'.

25 You can only ask us to consider a claim for special expenses if your injuries mean you have been unable to work or have been incapacitated for more than 28 weeks. However, if you qualify for special expenses we will pay them from the date of the actual injury. This is different from the loss of earnings rule, where we can pay only from week 29.

26 You can claim for damage to property or equipment belonging to you which you relied on as a physical aid and which was damaged in the incident. Examples would include walking sticks, spectacles and dentures. We will ask you for receipts for these.

27 The Scheme also covers expenses such as NHS prescriptions, dentists' and opticians' charges. We can consider meeting these costs only if you had to pay them yourself. Again, we will need proof of this. You may be able to get help for some of these costs from the NHS. You can get more information about this from:

Health Benefits Division
Sandyford House
Archbold Terrace
Newcastle-upon-Tyne
Tyne and Wear
NE2 1DB
Phone: **0191 203 5555**

28 We cannot meet costs if they can be met by the NHS.

29 The Scheme lets us consider paying the cost of private health treatment if both the treatment itself and its cost are reasonable in the circumstances of your case. It is not possible to define what is reasonable in any general way – it will vary from case to case. However, we will normally expect you to show that:

- the treatment you want is necessary and is proven to be effective;
- similarly effective treatment is not available on the NHS or otherwise available to you free of charge.

30 If we agree to cover the cost of such treatment, we will need to have receipts.

31 The Scheme deals with the cost of special equipment, adaptations to your home and caring for you (either at home or in a nursing home) when such care or equipment is appropriate to your injury. It is usually the most seriously injured applicants who make claims for this. If this applies to you or someone you are applying on behalf of, you might find these notes helpful.

- Special equipment covers physical aids (including specially-adapted vehicles, wheelchairs and walking aids), and kitchen implements to help people whose grip has weakened. If you have bought these, we will ask you for receipts. If you do not have a receipt, we will ask you to provide an estimate of their cost. Adaptations to your home can include changes both inside and outside your home (such as a ramp or a stair lift) to improve your ability to get around. We will only pay for items that are not available free of charge from your local authority, NHS or other agency.
- We can also compensate you for the cost of care relating to your bodily functions, or to the preparation of meals and supervision (to avoid sustantial risk to you and others). Again, we only consider claims for care which is not available free of charge. If a friend or a relative is caring for you at home, we will take account of any allowances that they receive, or could receive, to provide this care.

32 Since we can meet costs only if they cannot be met by the NHS or your local authority, we have to investigate what they are willing to provide. As we need to get clear information about this, we are likely to need your help.

33 There may be expenses you will need to meet more than once as a result of your injury. For example, you may need to replace equipment regularly. If so, we will use a process similar to that for working out future loss of earnings, involving a multiplicand and a multiplier, to produce a lump sum which will pay for these expenses in the future.

34 As with lost earnings, we must avoid any double payment. So, we have to reduce any award for special expenses to take account of social security benefits you receive or could receive to meet any of the same expenses. If the benefit is available to you, we have to take account of it, whether or not you choose to take it up. The Scheme says that if you could receive any social security or other state benefits, we may delay making an award until you have taken steps to claim them.

35 The rules on reducing awards to take account of insurance payments are more complicated. With loss of earnings we have to reduce the award if you have had payment for the same loss from an insurance policy which someone else paid for or contributed to, but not if you paid for it yourself. The same rules apply to claims for personal equipment such as spectacles, and the costs associated with NHS treatment. However, we also have to reduce your award to take account of insurance payments, even from a policy you

paid for yourself, if you are claiming for things like private health treatment, adaptations to your home or personal care.

APPENDIX 5 – TAKING ACCOUNT OF YOUR CRIMINAL RECORD

1 As we explained earlier, we will refuse or reduce an award if you have a criminal record. Even though you may have been blameless in the incident, the Scheme says that we must take account of your unspent criminal convictions.

2 It is often not easy to be sure whether or not a conviction is spent under the Rehabilitation of Offenders Act 1974. The more serious the penalty the offender received, and the more recently it was given, the longer the conviction will take to be spent. A conviction leading to a prison sentence of 30 months or more is never spent. There are more details in the Home Office leaflet 'Wiping the Slate Clean', which you can get by phoning our freephone number **0800 358 3601**.

3 The Scheme says we must reduce or refuse an award if someone has unspent convictions. When we decide to make an award to someone with a criminal record, we must use our discretion to decide what level of reduction will be appropriate. This is explained further below.

Penalty points system

4 Our current system of deciding about reductions is based on 'penalty points'. The more recent the conviction and the more serious the penalty, the more penalty points the conviction will attract. We will then use the number of penalty points to decide what level of reduction to make. We will also take account of any convictions you receive after the incident or after applying, right through to the date when your case is finally settled. The table on the next page shows how much unspent convictions may count against an award. In all cases, we ignore spent convictions.

5 Unless there are exceptional reasons, the percentage reductions we will consider for the various levels of penalty points are as follows:

Penalty points	*Percentage reduction*
1	10%
2	15%
3	25%
4	30%
5	35%
6	50%
7	60%
8	70%
9	80%
10	100%

6 We are not bound by the penalty-points system, but we must take account of all unspent convictions. The penalty points are our starting point, but we consider convictions and penalty points together with all the other circumstances of the application. For example, we may make a smaller reduction or no reduction at all, if you were injured while

helping the police uphold the law, or while helping someone who was being attacked. On the other hand, a low points score is no guarantee that we will make an award if, for example, your record includes violent or sexual offences.

Criminal convictions and fatal injuries

7 Where a victim has died, if either you (as the applicant) or the victim has a record of unspent criminal convictions, we have to take this into account.

8 We will pay funeral expenses in situations even if you have criminal convictions, but we may reduce or withhold an award if the victim had unspent criminal convictions.

	Court sentence		*Period between the date of the sentence and the date CICA receives the application*	*Penalty points*
1	Imprisonment for more than 30 months	a	Period of sentence or less	10
		b	More than (a) but less than sentence plus 5 years	9
		c	More than (b) but less than sentence plus 10 years	7
		d	More than sentence plus 10 years	5
2	Imprisonment for more than 6 months but not more than 30 months	a	Period of sentence or less	10
		b	More than (a) but less than sentence plus 3 years	8
		c	More than (b) but less than sentence plus 7 years	6
		d	More than sentence plus 7 years	2
3	Imprisonment for 6 months or less	a	Period of sentence or less	10
		b	More than (a) but less than sentence plus 2 years	5
		c	More than sentence plus 2 years	2
4	Fine over £250	a	Less than 2 years from sentence	3
		b	More than (a) but less than 3 years from sentence	2
		c	More than 3 years	1

	Court sentence	*Period between the date of the sentence and the date CICA receives the application*		*Penalty points*
5	Community Order, or another order or contract made as a penalty by the court	a	Period of the order or contract or less	3
		b	More than (a) and up to 2 years after the period of the order or contract	2
		c	More than 2 years after the period of the order or contract	1
6	Fine of £250 or less Compensation Order Conditional Discharge	a	Up to 2 years from sentence	2
		b	Over 2 years from sentence	1

Sentences given after you apply

9 We will treat sentences given after the date we get your application as if they had been given on the day before we receive the application.

More explanation about penalty points

- We count penalty points as shown in this table for all applications made under the 2008 Scheme.
- Imprisonment, whether suspended or not, means the sentence given by the court, not the time spent in prison.
- Imprisonment includes a sentence of detention in a young offenders' institution or other custodial sentence.
- Sentences spent under the Rehabilitation of Offenders Act 1974 do not attract penalty points.
- We will put other sentences into one of the six categories depending on how serious the offence is, as measured by the rehabilitation period set under the Rehabilitation of Offenders Act 1974.
- In the case of applications where someone has died, we will work out the points from the date of the sentence to the date the person died, not to the date we receive the application.

APPENDIX 6 – TARIFF OF INJURIES

[See the 2008 Scheme at **Appendix 1** for tables reproduced here]

Appendix 3
THE TRIBUNAL PROCEDURE (FIRST-TIER TRIBUNAL) (SOCIAL ENTITLEMENT CHAMBER) RULES 2008, SI 2008/2685

CONTENTS

After consulting in accordance with paragraph 28(1) of Schedule 5 to, the Tribunals, Courts and Enforcement Act 2007, the Tribunal Procedure Committee has made the following Rules in exercise of the powers conferred by sections 20(2) and (3) of the Social Security Act 1998 and sections 9(3), 22 and 29(3) of, and Schedule 5 to, the Tribunals, Courts and Enforcement Act 2007.

The Lord Chancellor has allowed the Rules in accordance with paragraph 28(3) of Schedule 5 to the Tribunals, Courts and Enforcement Act 2007.

PART 1 INTRODUCTION

Citation, commencement, application and interpretation

1. (1) These Rules may be cited as the Tribunal Procedure (First-tier Tribunal) (Social Entitlement Chamber) Rules 2008 and come into force on 3rd November 2008.
   (2) These Rules apply to proceedings before the Tribunal which have been assigned to the Social Entitlement Chamber by the First-tier Tribunal and Upper Tribunal (Chambers) Order 2008.
   (3) In these Rules –

   'the 2007 Act' means the Tribunals, Courts and Enforcement Act 2007;

'appeal' includes an application under section 19(9) of the Tax Credits Act 2002;

'appellant' means a person who makes an appeal to the Tribunal, or a person substituted as an appellant under rule 9(1) (substitution of parties);

'asylum support case' means proceedings concerning the provision of support for an asylum seeker, a failed asylum seeker or a person designated under section 130 of the Criminal Justice and Immigration Act 2008 (designation), or the dependents of any such person;

'criminal injuries compensation case' means proceedings concerning the payment of compensation under a scheme made under the Criminal Injuries Compensation Act 1995;

'decision maker' means the maker of a decision against which an appeal has been brought;

'dispose of proceedings' includes, unless indicated otherwise, disposing of a part of the proceedings;

'document' means anything in which information is recorded in any form, and an obligation under these Rules to provide or allow access to a document or a copy of a document for any purpose means, unless the Tribunal directs otherwise, an obligation to provide or allow access to such document or copy in a legible form or in a form which can be readily made into a legible form;

'hearing' means an oral hearing and includes a hearing conducted in whole or in part by video link, telephone or other means of instantaneous two-way electronic communication;

'legal representative' means a person who, for the purposes of the Legal Services Act 2007, is an authorised person in relation to an activity which constitutes the exercise of a right of audience or the conduct of litigation within the meaning of that Act, an advocate or solicitor in Scotland or a barrister or solicitor in Northern Ireland;

'party' means –

(a) a person who is an appellant or respondent in proceedings before the Tribunal;
(b) a person who makes a reference to the Tribunal under section 28D of the Child Support Act 1991;
(c) a person who starts proceedings before the Tribunal under paragraph 3 of Schedule 2 to the Tax Credits Act 2002; or
(d) if the proceedings have been concluded, a person who was a party under paragraph (a), (b) or (c) when the Tribunal finally disposed of all issues in the proceedings;

'practice direction' means a direction given under section 23 of the 2007 Act;

'respondent' means –

(a) in an appeal against a decision, the decision maker and any person other than the appellant who had a right of appeal against the decision;
(b) in a reference under section 28D of the Child Support Act 1991 –
    (i) the absent parent or non-resident parent;
    (ii) the person with care; and
    (iii) in Scotland, the child if the child made the application for a departure direction or a variation;

(c) in proceedings under paragraph 3 of Schedule 2 to the Tax Credits Act 2002, a person on whom it is proposed that a penalty be imposed; or
(d) a person substituted or added as a respondent under rule 9 (substitution and addition of parties);

'Social Entitlement Chamber' means the Social Entitlement Chamber of the First-tier Tribunal established by the First-tier Tribunal and Upper Tribunal (Chambers) Order 2008;

'social security and child support case' means any case allocated to the Social Entitlement Chamber except an asylum support case or a criminal injuries compensation case;

'Tribunal' means the First-tier Tribunal.

Overriding objective and parties' obligation to co-operate with the Tribunal

2. (1) The overriding objective of these Rules is to enable the Tribunal to deal with cases fairly and justly.
(2) Dealing with a case fairly and justly includes –
(a) dealing with the case in ways which are proportionate to the importance of the case, the complexity of the issues, the anticipated costs and the resources of the parties;
(b) avoiding unnecessary formality and seeking flexibility in the proceedings;
(c) ensuring, so far as practicable, that the parties are able to participate fully in the proceedings;
(d) using any special expertise of the Tribunal effectively; and
(e) avoiding delay, so far as compatible with proper consideration of the issues.
(3) The Tribunal must seek to give effect to the overriding objective when it –
(a) exercises any power under these Rules; or
(b) interprets any rule or practice direction.
(4) Parties must –
(a) help the Tribunal to further the overriding objective; and
(b) co-operate with the Tribunal generally.

Alternative dispute resolution and arbitration

3. (1) The Tribunal should seek, where appropriate –
(a) to bring to the attention of the parties the availability of any appropriate alternative procedure for the resolution of the dispute; and
(b) if the parties wish and provided that it is compatible with the overriding objective, to facilitate the use of the procedure.
(2) Part 1 of the Arbitration Act 1996 does not apply to proceedings before the Tribunal.

PART 2 GENERAL POWERS AND PROVISIONS

Delegation to staff

4. (1) Staff appointed under section 40(1) of the 2007 Act (tribunal staff and services) may, with the approval of the Senior President of Tribunals, carry out functions of a judicial nature permitted or required to be done by the Tribunal.
(2) The approval referred to at paragraph (1) may apply generally to the carrying

out of specified functions by members of staff of a specified description in specified circumstances.

(3) Within 14 days after the date on which the Tribunal sends notice of a decision made by a member of staff under paragraph (1) to a party, that party may apply in writing to the Tribunal for that decision to be considered afresh by a judge.

Case management powers

5. (1) Subject to the provisions of the 2007 Act and any other enactment, the Tribunal may regulate its own procedure.

(2) The Tribunal may give a direction in relation to the conduct or disposal of proceedings at any time, including a direction amending, suspending or setting aside an earlier direction.

(3) In particular, and without restricting the general powers in paragraphs (1) and (2), the Tribunal may –

(a) extend or shorten the time for complying with any rule, practice direction or direction;
(b) consolidate or hear together two or more sets of proceedings or parts of proceedings raising common issues, or treat a case as a lead case (whether in accordance with rule 18 (lead cases) or otherwise);
(c) permit or require a party to amend a document;
(d) permit or require a party or another person to provide documents, information, evidence or submissions to the Tribunal or a party;
(e) deal with an issue in the proceedings as a preliminary issue;
(f) hold a hearing to consider any matter, including a case management issue;
(g) decide the form of any hearing;
(h) adjourn or postpone a hearing;
(i) require a party to produce a bundle for a hearing;
(j) stay (or, in Scotland, sist) proceedings;
(k) transfer proceedings to another court or tribunal if that other court or tribunal has jurisdiction in relation to the proceedings and –

(i) because of a change of circumstances since the proceedings were started, the Tribunal no longer has jurisdiction in relation to the proceedings; or
(ii) the Tribunal considers that the other court or tribunal is a more appropriate forum for the determination of the case; or

(l) suspend the effect of its own decision pending the determination by the Tribunal or the Upper Tribunal of an application for permission to appeal against, and any appeal or review of, that decision.

Procedure for applying for and giving directions

6. (1) The Tribunal may give a direction on the application of one or more of the parties or on its own initiative.

(2) An application for a direction may be made –

(a) by sending or delivering a written application to the Tribunal; or
(b) orally during the course of a hearing.

(3) An application for a direction must include the reason for making that application.

(4) Unless the Tribunal considers that there is good reason not to do so, the Tribunal must send written notice of any direction to every party and to any other person affected by the direction.

(5) If a party or any other person sent notice of the direction under paragraph (4)

wishes to challenge a direction which the Tribunal has given, they may do so by applying for another direction which amends, suspends or sets aside the first direction.

Failure to comply with rules etc.

7. (1) An irregularity resulting from a failure to comply with any requirement in these Rules, a practice direction or a direction, does not of itself render void the proceedings or any step taken in the proceedings.

(2) If a party has failed to comply with a requirement in these Rules, a practice direction or a direction, the Tribunal may take such action as it considers just, which may include –

(a) waiving the requirement;
(b) requiring the failure to be remedied;
(c) exercising its power under rule 8 (striking out a party's case); or
(d) exercising its power under paragraph (3).

(3) The Tribunal may refer to the Upper Tribunal, and ask the Upper Tribunal to exercise its power under section 25 of the 2007 Act in relation to, any failure by a person to comply with a requirement imposed by the Tribunal –

(a) to attend at any place for the purpose of giving evidence;
(b) otherwise to make themselves available to give evidence;
(c) to swear an oath in connection with the giving of evidence;
(d) to give evidence as a witness;
(e) to produce a document; or
(f) to facilitate the inspection of a document or any other thing (including any premises).

Striking out a party's case

8. (1) The proceedings, or the appropriate part of them, will automatically be struck out if the appellant has failed to comply with a direction that stated that failure by a party to comply with the direction would lead to the striking out of the proceedings or that part of them.

(2) The Tribunal must strike out the whole or a part of the proceedings if the Tribunal –

(a) does not have jurisdiction in relation to the proceedings or that part of them; and
(b) does not exercise its power under rule 5(3)(k)(i) (transfer to another court or tribunal) in relation to the proceedings or that part of them.

(3) The Tribunal may strike out the whole or a part of the proceedings if –

(a) the appellant has failed to comply with a direction which stated that failure by the appellant to comply with the direction could lead to the striking out of the proceedings or part of them;
(b) the appellant has failed to co-operate with the Tribunal to such an extent that the Tribunal cannot deal with the proceedings fairly and justly; or
(c) the Tribunal considers there is no reasonable prospect of the appellant's case, or part of it, succeeding.

(4) The Tribunal may not strike out the whole or a part of the proceedings under paragraph (2) or (3)(b) or (c) without first giving the appellant an opportunity to make representations in relation to the proposed striking out.

(5) If the proceedings, or part of them, have been struck out under paragraph (1) or (3)(a), the appellant may apply for the proceedings, or part of them, to be reinstated.

(6) An application under paragraph (5) must be made in writing and received by the Tribunal within 1 month after the date on which the Tribunal sent notification of the striking out to the appellant.

(7) This rule applies to a respondent as it applies to an appellant except that –

(a) a reference to the striking out of the proceedings is to be read as a reference to the barring of the respondent from taking further part in the proceedings; and

(b) a reference to an application for the reinstatement of proceedings which have been struck out is to be read as a reference to an application for the lifting of the bar on the respondent from taking further part in the proceedings.

(8) If a respondent has been barred from taking further part in proceedings under this rule and that bar has not been lifted, the Tribunal need not consider any response or other submission made by that respondent.

Substitution and addition of parties

9. (1) The Tribunal may give a direction substituting a party if –

(a) the wrong person has been named as a party; or

(b) the substitution has become necessary because of a change in circumstances since the start of proceedings.

(2) The Tribunal may give a direction adding a person to the proceedings as a respondent.

(3) If the Tribunal gives a direction under paragraph (1) or (2) it may give such consequential directions as it considers appropriate.

No power to award costs

10. The Tribunal may not make any order in respect of costs (or, in Scotland, expenses).

Representatives

11. (1) A party may appoint a representative (whether a legal representative or not) to represent that party in the proceedings.

(2) Subject to paragraph (3), if a party appoints a representative, that party (or the representative if the representative is a legal representative) must send or deliver to the Tribunal written notice of the representative's name and address.

(3) In a case to which rule 23 (cases in which the notice of appeal is to be sent to the decision maker) applies, if the appellant (or the appellant's representative if the representative is a legal representative) provides written notification of the appellant's representative's name and address to the decision maker before the decision maker provides its response to the Tribunal, the appellant need not take any further steps in order to comply with paragraph (2).

(4) If the Tribunal receives notice that a party has appointed a representative under paragraph (2), it must send a copy of that notice to each other party.

(5) Anything permitted or required to be done by a party under these Rules, a practice direction or a direction may be done by the representative of that party, except signing a witness statement.

(6) A person who receives due notice of the appointment of a representative –

(a) must provide to the representative any document which is required to be provided to the represented party, and need not provide that document to the represented party; and

(b) may assume that the representative is and remains authorised as such until they receive written notification that this is not so from the representative or the represented party.

(7) At a hearing a party may be accompanied by another person whose name and address has not been notified under paragraph (2) or (3) but who, with the permission of the Tribunal, may act as a representative or otherwise assist in presenting the party's case at the hearing.

(8) Paragraphs (2) to (6) do not apply to a person who accompanies a party under paragraph (7).

Calculating time

12\. (1) Except in asylum support cases, an act required by these Rules, a practice direction or a direction to be done on or by a particular day must be done by 5pm on that day.

(2) If the time specified by these Rules, a practice direction or a direction for doing any act ends on a day other than a working day, the act is done in time if it is done on the next working day.

(3) In this rule 'working day' means any day except a Saturday or Sunday, Christmas Day, Good Friday or a bank holiday under section 1 of the Banking and Financial Dealings Act 1971.

Sending and delivery of documents

13\. (1) Any document to be provided to the Tribunal under these Rules, a practice direction or a direction must be –

(a) sent by pre-paid post or delivered by hand to the address specified for the proceedings;
(b) sent by fax to the number specified for the proceedings; or
(c) sent or delivered by such other method as the Tribunal may permit or direct.

(2) Subject to paragraph (3), if a party provides a fax number, email address or other details for the electronic transmission of documents to them, that party must accept delivery of documents by that method.

(3) If a party informs the Tribunal and all other parties that a particular form of communication (other than pre-paid post or delivery by hand) should not be used to provide documents to that party, that form of communication must not be so used.

(4) If the Tribunal or a party sends a document to a party or the Tribunal by email or any other electronic means of communication, the recipient may request that the sender provide a hard copy of the document to the recipient. The recipient must make such a request as soon as reasonably practicable after receiving the document electronically.

(5) The Tribunal and each party may assume that the address provided by a party or its representative is and remains the address to which documents should be sent or delivered until receiving written notification to the contrary.

Use of documents and information

14\. (1) The Tribunal may make an order prohibiting the disclosure or publication of –

(a) specified documents or information relating to the proceedings; or
(b) any matter likely to lead members of the public to identify any person whom the Tribunal considers should not be identified.

(2) The Tribunal may give a direction prohibiting the disclosure of a document or information to a person if –

(a) the Tribunal is satisfied that such disclosure would be likely to cause that person or some other person serious harm; and
(b) the Tribunal is satisfied, having regard to the interests of justice, that it is proportionate to give such a direction.

(3) If a party ('the first party') considers that the Tribunal should give a direction under paragraph (2) prohibiting the disclosure of a document or information to another party ('the second party'), the first party must –

(a) exclude the relevant document or information from any documents that will be provided to the second party; and
(b) provide to the Tribunal the excluded document or information, and the reason for its exclusion, so that the Tribunal may decide whether the document or information should be disclosed to the second party or should be the subject of a direction under paragraph (2).

(4) The Tribunal must conduct proceedings as appropriate in order to give effect to a direction given under paragraph (2).

(5) If the Tribunal gives a direction under paragraph (2) which prevents disclosure to a party who has appointed a representative, the Tribunal may give a direction that the documents or information be disclosed to that representative if the Tribunal is satisfied that –

(a) disclosure to the representative would be in the interests of the party; and
(b) the representative will act in accordance with paragraph (6).

(6) Documents or information disclosed to a representative in accordance with a direction under paragraph (5) must not be disclosed either directly or indirectly to any other person without the Tribunal's consent.

Evidence and submissions

15. (1) Without restriction on the general powers in rule 5(1) and (2) (case management powers), the Tribunal may give directions as to –

(a) issues on which it requires evidence or submissions;
(b) the nature of the evidence or submissions it requires;
(c) whether the parties are permitted or required to provide expert evidence;
(d) any limit on the number of witnesses whose evidence a party may put forward, whether in relation to a particular issue or generally;
(e) the manner in which any evidence or submissions are to be provided, which may include a direction for them to be given –

(i) orally at a hearing; or
(ii) by written submissions or witness statement; and

(f) the time at which any evidence or submissions are to be provided.

(2) The Tribunal may –

(a) admit evidence whether or not –

(i) the evidence would be admissible in a civil trial in the United Kingdom; or
(ii) the evidence was available to a previous decision maker; or

(b) exclude evidence that would otherwise be admissible where –

(i) the evidence was not provided within the time allowed by a direction or a practice direction;
(ii) the evidence was otherwise provided in a manner that did not comply with a direction or a practice direction; or
(iii) it would otherwise be unfair to admit the evidence.

(3) The Tribunal may consent to a witness giving, or require any witness to give, evidence on oath, and may administer an oath for that purpose.

Summoning or citation of witnesses and orders to answer questions or produce documents

16. (1) On the application of a party or on its own initiative, the Tribunal may –

(a) by summons (or, in Scotland, citation) require any person to attend as a witness at a hearing at the time and place specified in the summons or citation; or

(b) order any person to answer any questions or produce any documents in that person's possession or control which relate to any issue in the proceedings.

(2) A summons or citation under paragraph (1)(a) must –

(a) give the person required to attend 14 days' notice of the hearing or such shorter period as the Tribunal may direct; and

(b) where the person is not a party, make provision for the person's necessary expenses of attendance to be paid, and state who is to pay them.

(3) No person may be compelled to give any evidence or produce any document that the person could not be compelled to give or produce on a trial of an action in a court of law in the part of the United Kingdom where the proceedings are due to be determined.

(4) A summons, citation or order under this rule must –

(a) state that the person on whom the requirement is imposed may apply to the Tribunal to vary or set aside the summons, citation or order, if they have not had an opportunity to object to it; and

(b) state the consequences of failure to comply with the summons, citation or order.

Withdrawal

17. (1) Subject to paragraph (2), a party may give notice of the withdrawal of its case, or any part of it –

(a) at any time before a hearing to consider the disposal of the proceedings (or, if the Tribunal disposes of the proceedings without a hearing, before that disposal), by sending or delivering to the Tribunal a written notice of withdrawal; or

(b) orally at a hearing.

(2) In the circumstances described in paragraph (3), a notice of withdrawal will not take effect unless the Tribunal consents to the withdrawal.

(3) The circumstances referred to in paragraph (2) are where a party gives notice of withdrawal –

(a) under paragraph (1)(a) in a criminal injuries compensation case; or

(b) under paragraph (1)(b).

(4) A party who has withdrawn their case may apply to the Tribunal for the case to be reinstated.

(5) An application under paragraph (4) must be made in writing and be received by the Tribunal within 1 month after –

(a) the date on which the Tribunal received the notice under paragraph (1)(a); or

(b) the date of the hearing at which the case was withdrawn orally under paragraph (1)(b).

(6) The Tribunal must notify each party in writing of an withdrawal under this rule.

Lead cases

18. (1) This rule applies if –

(a) two or more cases have been started before the Tribunal;
(b) in each such case the Tribunal has not made a decision disposing of the proceedings; and
(c) the cases give rise to common or related issues of fact or law.

(2) The Tribunal may give a direction –

(a) specifying one or more cases falling under paragraph (1) as a lead case or lead cases; and
(b) staying (or, in Scotland, sisting) the other cases falling under paragraph (1) ('the related cases').

(3) When the Tribunal makes a decision in respect of the common or related issues –

(a) the Tribunal must send a copy of that decision to each party in each of the related cases; and
(b) subject to paragraph (4), that decision shall be binding on each of those parties.

(4) Within 1 month after the date on which the Tribunal sent a copy of the decision to a party under paragraph (3)(a), that party may apply in writing for a direction that the decision does not apply to, and is not binding on the parties to, a particular related case.

(5) The Tribunal must give directions in respect of cases which are stayed or sisted under paragraph (2)(b), providing for the disposal of or further directions in those cases.

(6) If the lead case or cases lapse or are withdrawn before the Tribunal makes a decision in respect of the common or related issues, the Tribunal must give directions as to –

(a) whether another case or other cases are to be specified as a lead case or lead cases; and
(b) whether any direction affecting the related cases should be set aside or amended.

Confidentiality in child support or child trust fund cases

19. (1) Paragraph (3) applies to proceedings under the Child Support Act 1991 in the circumstances described in paragraph (2), other than an appeal against a reduced benefit decision (as defined in section 46(10)(b) of the Child Support Act 1991, as that section had effect prior to the commencement of section 15(b) of the Child Maintenance and Other Payments Act 2008).

(2) The circumstances referred to in paragraph (1) are that the absent parent, non-resident parent or person with care would like their address or the address of the child to be kept confidential and has given notice to that effect –

(a) to the Secretary of State or the Child Maintenance and Enforcement Commission in the notice of appeal or when notifying any subsequent change of address;
(b) to the Secretary of State or the Child Maintenance and Enforcement

Commission, whichever has made the enquiry, within 14 days after an enquiry is made; or
(c) to the Tribunal when notifying any change of address.

(3) Where this paragraph applies, the Secretary of State, the Child Maintenance and Enforcement Commission and the Tribunal must take appropriate steps to secure the confidentiality of the address, and of any information which could reasonably be expected to enable a person to identify the address, to the extent that the address or that information is not already known to each other party.

(4) Paragraph (6) applies to proceedings under the Child Trust Funds Act 2004 in the circumstances described in paragraph (5).

(5) The circumstances referred to in paragraph (4) are that a relevant person would like their address or the address of the eligible child to be kept confidential and has given notice to that effect, or a local authority with parental responsibility in relation to the eligible child would like the address of the eligible child to be kept confidential and has given notice to that effect –

(a) to HMRC in the notice of appeal or when notifying any subsequent change of address;
(b) to HMRC within 14 days after an enquiry by HMRC; or
(c) to the Tribunal when notifying any change of address.

(6) Where this paragraph applies, HMRC and the Tribunal must take appropriate steps to secure the confidentiality of the address, and of any information which could reasonably be expected to enable a person to identify the address, to the extent that the address or that information is not already known to each other party.

(7) In this rule –

'eligible child' has the meaning set out in section 2 of the Child Trust Funds Act 2004;

'HMRC' means Her Majesty's Revenue and Customs;

'non-resident parent' and 'parent with care' have the meanings set out in section 54 of the Child Support Act 1991;

'parental responsibility' has the meaning set out in section 3(9) of the Child Trust Funds Act 2004; and

'relevant person' has the meaning set out in section 22(3) of the Child Trust Funds Act 2004.

Expenses in criminal injuries compensation cases

20\. (1) This rule applies only to criminal injuries compensation cases.

(2) The Tribunal may meet reasonable expenses –

(a) incurred by the appellant, or any person who attends a hearing to give evidence, in attending the hearing; or
(b) incurred by the appellant in connection with any arrangements made by the Tribunal for the inspection of the appellant's injury.

Expenses in social security and child support cases

21\. (1) This rule applies only to social security and child support cases.

(2) The Secretary of State may pay such travelling and other allowances (including compensation for loss of remunerative time) as the Secretary of State may determine to any person required to attend a hearing in proceedings under section 20 of the Child Support Act 1991, section 12 of the Social Security Act 1998 or paragraph 6 of Schedule 7 to the Child Support, Pensions and Social Security Act 2000.

PART 3 PROCEEDINGS BEFORE THE TRIBUNAL

CHAPTER 1 BEFORE THE HEARING

Cases in which the notice of appeal is to be sent to the Tribunal

22. (1) This rule applies to asylum support cases and criminal injuries compensation cases.

(2) An appellant must start proceedings by sending or delivering a notice of appeal to the Tribunal so that it is received –

(a) in asylum support cases, within 3 days after the date on which the appellant received written notice of the decision being challenged;
(b) in criminal injuries compensation cases, within 90 days after the date of the decision being challenged.

(3) The notice of appeal must be in English or Welsh, must be signed by the appellant and must state –

(a) the name and address of the appellant;
(b) the name and address of the appellant's representative (if any);
(c) an address where documents for the appellant may be sent or delivered;
(d) the name and address of any respondent;
(e) details (including the full reference) of the decision being appealed; and
(f) the grounds on which the appellant relies.

(4) The appellant must provide with the notice of appeal –

(a) a copy of any written record of the decision being challenged;
(b) any statement of reasons for that decision that the appellant has or can reasonably obtain;
(c) any documents in support of the appellant's case which have not been supplied to the respondent; and
(d) any further information or documents required by an applicable practice direction.

(5) In asylum support cases the notice of appeal must also –

(a) state whether the appellant will require an interpreter at any hearing, and if so for which language or dialect; and
(b) state whether the appellant intends to attend or be represented at any hearing.

(6) If the appellant provides the notice of appeal to the Tribunal later than the time required by paragraph (2) or by an extension of time allowed under rule 5(3)(a) (power to extend time) –

(a) the notice of appeal must include a request for an extension of time and the reason why the notice of appeal was not provided in time; and
(b) unless the Tribunal extends time for the notice of appeal under rule 5(3)(a) (power to extend time) the Tribunal must not admit the notice of appeal.

(7) The Tribunal must send a copy of the notice of appeal and any accompanying documents to each other party –

(a) in asylum support cases, on the day that the Tribunal receives the notice of appeal, or (if that is not reasonably practicable) as soon as reasonably practicable on the following day;
(b) in criminal injuries compensation cases, as soon as reasonably practicable after the Tribunal receives the notice of appeal.

Cases in which the notice of appeal is to be sent to the decision maker

23. (1) This rule applies to social security and child support cases (except references under the Child Support Act 1991 and proceedings under paragraph 3 of Schedule 2 to the Tax Credits Act 2002).

(2) An appellant must start proceedings by sending or delivering a notice of appeal to the decision maker so that it is received within the time specified in Schedule 1 to these Rules (time limits for providing notices of appeal to the decision maker).

(3) If the appellant provides the notice of appeal to the decision maker later than the time required by paragraph (2) the notice of appeal must include the reason why the notice of appeal was not provided in time.

(4) Subject to paragraph (5), where an appeal is not made within the time specified in Schedule 1, it will be treated as having been made in time if the decision maker does not object.

(5) No appeal may be made more than 12 months after the time specified in Schedule 1.

(6) The notice of appeal must be in English or Welsh, must be signed by the appellant and must state –

(a) the name and address of the appellant;
(b) the name and address of the appellant's representative (if any);
(c) an address where documents for the appellant may be sent or delivered;
(d) details of the decision being appealed; and
(e) the grounds on which the appellant relies.

(7) The decision maker must refer the case to the Tribunal immediately if –

(a) the appeal has been made after the time specified in Schedule 1 and the decision maker objects to it being treated as having been made in time; or
(b) the decision maker considers that the appeal has been made more than 12 months after the time specified in Schedule 1.

(8) Notwithstanding rule 5(3)(a) (case management powers) and rule 7(2) (failure to comply with rules etc.), the Tribunal must not extend the time limit in paragraph (5).

Responses and replies

24. (1) When a decision maker receives the notice of appeal or a copy of it, the decision maker must send or deliver a response to the Tribunal –

(a) in asylum support cases, so that it is received within 3 days after the date on which the Tribunal received the notice of appeal; and
(b) in other cases, as soon as reasonably practicable after the decision maker received the notice of appeal.

(2) The response must state –

(a) the name and address of the decision maker;
(b) the name and address of the decision maker's representative (if any);
(c) an address where documents for the decision maker may be sent or delivered;
(d) the names and addresses of any other respondents and their representatives (if any);
(e) whether the decision maker opposes the appellant's case and, if so, any grounds for such opposition which are not set out in any documents which are before the Tribunal; and
(f) any further information or documents required by a practice direction or direction.

(3) The response may include a submission as to whether it would be appropriate for the case to be disposed of without a hearing.

(4) The decision maker must provide with the response –

(a) a copy of any written record of the decision under challenge, and any statement of reasons for that decision, if they were not sent with the notice of appeal;

(b) copies of all documents relevant to the case in the decision maker's possession, unless a practice direction or direction states otherwise; and

(c) in cases to which rule 23 (cases in which the notice of appeal is to be sent to the decision maker) applies, a copy of the notice of appeal, any documents provided by the appellant with the notice of appeal and (if they have not otherwise been provided to the Tribunal) the name and address of the appellant's representative (if any).

(5) The decision maker must provide a copy of the response and any accompanying documents to each other party at the same time as it provides the response to the Tribunal.

(6) The appellant and any other respondent may make a written submission and supply further documents in reply to the decision maker's response.

(7) Any submission or further documents under paragraph (6) must be provided to the Tribunal within 1 month after the date on which the decision maker sent the response to the party providing the reply, and the Tribunal must send a copy to each other party.

Medical and physical examination in appeals under section 12 of the Social Security Act 1998

25\. (1) This rule applies only to appeals under section 12 of the Social Security Act 1998.

(2) At a hearing an appropriate member of the Tribunal may carry out a physical examination of a person if the case relates to –

(a) the extent of that person's disablement and its assessment in accordance with section 68(6) of and Schedule 6 to, or section 103 of, the Social Security Contributions and Benefits Act 1992; or

(b) diseases or injuries prescribed for the purpose of section 108 of that Act.

(3) If an issue which falls within Schedule 2 to these Rules (issues in relation to which the Tribunal may refer a person for medical examination) is raised in an appeal, the Tribunal may exercise its power under section 20 of the Social Security Act 1998 to refer a person to a health care professional approved by the Secretary of State for –

(a) the examination of that person; and

(b) the production of a report on the condition of that person.

(4) Neither paragraph (2) nor paragraph (3) entitles the Tribunal to require a person to undergo a physical test for the purpose of determining whether that person is unable to walk or virtually unable to do so.

Social security and child support cases started by reference or information in writing

26\. (1) This rule applies to proceedings under section 28D of the Child Support Act 1991 and paragraph 3 of Schedule 2 to the Tax Credits Act 2002.

(2) A person starting proceedings under section 28D of the Child Support Act 1991 must send or deliver a written reference to the Tribunal.

(3) A person starting proceedings under paragraph 3 of Schedule 2 to the Tax Credits Act 2002 must send or deliver an information in writing to the Tribunal.

(4) The reference or the information in writing must include –

(a) an address where documents for the person starting proceedings may be sent or delivered;
(b) the names and addresses of the respondents and their representatives (if any); and
(c) a submission on the issues that arise for determination by the Tribunal.

(5) Unless a practice direction or direction states otherwise, the person starting proceedings must also provide a copy of each document in their possession which is relevant to the proceedings.

(6) Subject to any obligation under rule 19(3) (confidentiality in child support cases), the person starting proceedings must provide a copy of the written reference or the information in writing and any accompanying documents to each respondent at the same time as they provide the written reference or the information in writing to the Tribunal.

(7) Each respondent may send or deliver to the Tribunal a written submission and any further relevant documents within one month of the date on which the person starting proceedings sent a copy of the written reference or the information in writing to that respondent.

CHAPTER 2 HEARINGS

Decision with or without a hearing

27. (1) Subject to the following paragraphs, the Tribunal must hold a hearing before making a decision which disposes of proceedings unless –

(a) each party has consented to, or has not objected to, the matter being decided without a hearing; and
(b) the Tribunal considers that it is able to decide the matter without a hearing.

(2) This rule does not apply to decisions under Part 4.

(3) The Tribunal may in any event dispose of proceedings without a hearing under rule 8 (striking out a party's case).

(4) In a criminal injuries compensation case –

(a) the Tribunal may make a decision which disposes of proceedings without a hearing; and
(b) subject to paragraph (5), if the Tribunal makes a decision which disposes of proceedings without a hearing, any party may make a written application to the Tribunal for the decision to be reconsidered at a hearing.

(5) An application under paragraph (4)(b) may not be made in relation to a decision –

(a) not to extend a time limit;
(b) not to set aside a previous decision;
(c) not to allow an appeal against a decision not to extend a time limit; or
(d) not to allow an appeal against a decision not to reopen a case.

(6) An application under paragraph (4)(b) must be received within 1 month after the date on which the Tribunal sent notice of the decision to the party making the application.

Entitlement to attend a hearing

28. Subject to rule 30(5) (exclusion of a person from a hearing), each party to proceedings is entitled to attend a hearing.

Notice of hearings

29. (1) The Tribunal must give each party entitled to attend a hearing reasonable notice of the time and place of the hearing (including any adjourned or postponed hearing) and any changes to the time and place of the hearing.
 (2) The period of notice under paragraph (1) must be at least 14 days except that –
 (a) in an asylum support case the Tribunal must give at least 1 day's and not more than 5 days' notice; and
 (b) the Tribunal may give shorter notice –
 (i) with the parties' consent; or
 (ii) in urgent or exceptional circumstances.

Public and private hearings

30. (1) Subject to the following paragraphs, all hearings must be held in public.
 (2) A hearing in a criminal injuries compensation case must be held in private unless –
 (a) the appellant has consented to the hearing being held in public; and
 (b) the Tribunal considers that it is in the interests of justice for the hearing to be held in public.
 (3) The Tribunal may give a direction that a hearing, or part of it, is to be held in private.
 (4) Where a hearing, or part of it, is to be held in private, the Tribunal may determine who is permitted to attend the hearing or part of it.
 (5) The Tribunal may give a direction excluding from any hearing, or part of it –
 (a) any person whose conduct the Tribunal considers is disrupting or is likely to disrupt the hearing;
 (b) any person whose presence the Tribunal considers is likely to prevent another person from giving evidence or making submissions freely;
 (c) any person who the Tribunal considers should be excluded in order to give effect to a direction under rule 14(2) (withholding information likely to cause harm); or
 (d) any person where the purpose of the hearing would be defeated by the attendance of that person.
 (6) The Tribunal may give a direction excluding a witness from a hearing until that witness gives evidence.

Hearings in a party's absence

31. If a party fails to attend a hearing the Tribunal may proceed with the hearing if the Tribunal –
 (a) is satisfied that the party has been notified of the hearing or that reasonable steps have been taken to notify the party of the hearing; and
 (b) considers that it is in the interests of justice to proceed with the hearing.

CHAPTER 3 DECISIONS

Consent orders

32. (1) The Tribunal may, at the request of the parties but only if it considers it appropriate, make a consent order disposing of the proceedings and making such other appropriate provision as the parties have agreed.

(2) Notwithstanding any other provision of these Rules, the Tribunal need not hold a hearing before making an order under paragraph (1), or provide reasons for the order.

Notice of decisions

33. (1) The Tribunal may give a decision orally at a hearing.

(2) Subject to rule 14(2) (withholding information likely to cause harm), the Tribunal must provide to each party as soon as reasonably practicable after making a decision which finally disposes of all issues in the proceedings (except a decision under Part 4) –

(a) a decision notice stating the Tribunal's decision;

(b) where appropriate, notification of the right to apply for a written statement of reasons under rule 34(3); and

(c) notification of any right of appeal against the decision and the time within which, and the manner in which, such right of appeal may be exercised.

(3) In asylum support cases the notice and notifications required by paragraph (2) must be provided at the hearing or sent on the day that the decision is made.

Reasons for decisions

34. (1) In asylum support cases the Tribunal must send a written statement of reasons for a decision which disposes of proceedings (except a decision under Part 4) to each party –

(a) if the case is decided at a hearing, within 3 days after the hearing; or

(b) if the case is decided without a hearing, on the day that the decision is made.

(2) In all other cases the Tribunal may give reasons for a decision which disposes of proceedings (except a decision under Part 4) –

(a) orally at a hearing; or

(b) in a written statement of reasons to each party.

(3) Unless the Tribunal has already provided a written statement of reasons under paragraph (2)(b), a party may make a written application to the Tribunal for such statement following a decision which finally disposes of all issues in the proceedings.

(4) An application under paragraph (3) must be received within 1 month of the date on which the Tribunal sent or otherwise provided to the party a decision notice relating to the decision which finally disposes of all issues in the proceedings.

(5) If a party makes an application in accordance with paragraphs (3) and (4) the Tribunal must, subject to rule 14(2) (withholding information likely to cause harm), send a written statement of reasons to each party within 1 month of the date on which it received the application or as soon as reasonably practicable after the end of that period.

PART 4 CORRECTING, SETTING ASIDE, REVIEWING AND APPEALING TRIBUNAL DECISIONS

Interpretation

35. In this Part –

'appeal' means the exercise of a right of appeal –

(a) under paragraph 2(2) or 4(1) of Schedule 2 to the Tax Credits Act 2002;
(b) under section 21(10) of the Child Trust Funds Act 2004; or
(c) on a point of law under section 11 of the 2007 Act; and

'review' means the review of a decision by the Tribunal under section 9 of the 2007 Act.

Clerical mistakes and accidental slips or omissions

36. The Tribunal may at any time correct any clerical mistake or other accidental slip or omission in a decision, direction or any document produced by it, by –

(a) sending notification of the amended decision or direction, or a copy of the amended document, to all parties; and
(b) making any necessary amendment to any information published in relation to the decision, direction or document.

Setting aside a decision which disposes of proceedings

37. (1) The Tribunal may set aside a decision which disposes of proceedings, or part of such a decision, and re-make the decision, or the relevant part of it, if –

(a) the Tribunal considers that it is in the interests of justice to do so; and
(b) one or more of the conditions in paragraph (2) are satisfied.

(2) The conditions are –

(a) a document relating to the proceedings was not sent to, or was not received at an appropriate time by, a party or a party's representative;
(b) a document relating to the proceedings was not sent to the Tribunal at an appropriate time;
(c) a party, or a party's representative, was not present at a hearing related to the proceedings; or
(d) there has been some other procedural irregularity in the proceedings.

(3) A party applying for a decision, or part of a decision, to be set aside under paragraph (1) must make a written application to the Tribunal so that it is received no later than 1 month after the date on which the Tribunal sent notice of the decision to the party.

Application for permission to appeal

38. (1) This rule does not apply to asylum support cases or criminal injuries compensation cases.

(2) A person seeking permission to appeal must make a written application to the Tribunal for permission to appeal.

(3) An application under paragraph (2) must be sent or delivered to the Tribunal so that it is received no later than 1 month after the latest of the dates that the Tribunal sends to the person making the application –

(a) written reasons for the decision;
(b) notification of amended reasons for, or correction of, the decision following a review; or
(c) notification that an application for the decision to be set aside has been unsuccessful.

(4) The date in paragraph (3)(c) applies only if the application for the decision to be set aside was made within the time stipulated in rule 37 (setting aside a decision which disposes of proceedings) or any extension of that time granted by the Tribunal.

(5) If the person seeking permission to appeal sends or delivers the application to

the Tribunal later than the time required by paragraph (3) or by any extension of time under rule 5(3)(a) (power to extend time) –

(a) the application must include a request for an extension of time and the reason why the application was not provided in time; and
(b) unless the Tribunal extends time for the application under rule 5(3)(a) (power to extend time) the Tribunal must not admit the application.

(6) An application under paragraph (2) must –

(a) identify the decision of the Tribunal to which it relates;
(b) identify the alleged error or errors of law in the decision; and
(c) state the result the party making the application is seeking.

(7) If a person makes an application under paragraph (2) when the Tribunal has not given a written statement of reasons for its decision –

(a) if no application for a written statement of reasons has been made to the Tribunal, the application for permission must be treated as such an application;
(b) unless the Tribunal decides to give permission and directs that this sub-paragraph does not apply, the application is not to be treated as an application for permission to appeal; and
(c) if an application for a written statement of reasons has been, or is, refused because of a delay in making the application, the Tribunal must only admit the application for permission if the Tribunal considers that it is in the interests of justice to do so.

Tribunal's consideration of application for permission to appeal

39. (1) On receiving an application for permission to appeal the Tribunal must first consider, taking into account the overriding objective in rule 2, whether to review the decision in accordance with rule 40 (review of a decision).

(2) If the Tribunal decides not to review the decision, or reviews the decision and decides to take no action in relation to the decision, or part of it, the Tribunal must consider whether to give permission to appeal in relation to the decision or that part of it.

(3) The Tribunal must send a record of its decision to the parties as soon as practicable.

(4) If the Tribunal refuses permission to appeal it must send with the record of its decision –

(a) a statement of its reasons for such refusal; and
(b) notification of the right to make an application to the Upper Tribunal for permission to appeal and the time within which, and the method by which, such application must be made.

(5) The Tribunal may give permission to appeal on limited grounds, but must comply with paragraph (4) in relation to any grounds on which it has refused permission.

Review of a decision

40. (1) This rule does not apply to asylum support cases or criminal injuries compensation cases.

(2) The Tribunal may only undertake a review of a decision –

(a) pursuant to rule 39(1) (review on an application for permission to appeal); and
(b) if it is satisfied that there was an error of law in the decision.

(3) The Tribunal must notify the parties in writing of the outcome of any review, and of any right of appeal in relation to the outcome.

(4) If the Tribunal takes any action in relation to a decision following a review without first giving every party an opportunity to make representations, the notice under paragraph (3) must state that any party that did not have an opportunity to make representations may apply for such action to be set aside and for the decision to be reviewed again.

Power to treat an application as a different type of application

41. The Tribunal may treat an application for a decision to be corrected, set aside or reviewed, or for permission to appeal against a decision, as an application for any other one of those things.

Patrick Elias
Phillip Brook Smith Q.C.
Lesley Clare
Douglas J. May Q.C.
Newton of Braintree
M.J. Reed
Mark Rowland
Nicholas Warren

I allow these Rules
Signed by authority of the Lord Chancellor

Bridget Prentice
Parliamentary Under Secretary of State
Ministry of Justice

9th October 2008

SCHEDULE 1 TIME LIMITS FOR PROVIDING NOTICES OF APPEAL TO THE DECISION MAKER

Rule 23

Type of proceedings	*Time for providing notice of appeal*
cases other than those listed below	the latest of – (a) one month after the date on which notice of the decision being challenged was sent to the appellant; (b) if a written statement of reasons for the decision is requested, 14 days after the later of (i) the date on which the period at (a) expires; and (ii) the date on which the written statement of reasons was provided; or (c) where the appellant made an application for revision of the decision under –

	(i) regulation 17(1)(a) of the Child Support (Maintenance Assessment Procedure) Regulations 1992; (ii) regulation 3(1) or (3) or 3A(1) of the Social Security and Child Support (Decision & Appeals) Regulations 1999; or (iii) regulation 4 of the Housing Benefit and Council Tax Benefit (Decisions and Appeals) Regulations 2001 and that application was unsuccessful, one month of the date on which notice that the decision would not be revised was sent to the appellant
appeal against a certificate of NHS charges under section 157(1) of the Health and Social Care (Community Health and Standards) Act 2003	(a) 3 months after the latest of – (i) the date on the certificate; (ii) the date on which the compensation payment was made; (iii) if the certificate has been reviewed, the date the certificate was confirmed or a fresh certificate was issued; or (iv) the date of any agreement to treat an earlier compensation payment as having been made in final discharge of a claim made by or in respect of an injured person and arising out of the injury or death; or (b) if the person to whom the certificate has been issued makes an application under section 157(4) of the Health and Social Care (Community Health and Standards) Act 2003, one month after – (i) the date of the decision on that application; or (ii) if the person appeals against that decision under section 157(6) of that Act, the date on which the appeal is decided or withdrawn
appeal against a waiver decision under section 157(6) of the Health and Social Care (Community Health and Standards) Act 2003	one month after the date of the decision

appeal against a certificate of NHS charges under section 7 of the Road Traffic (NHS Charges) Act 1999	3 months after the latest of – (a) the date on which the liability under section 1(2) of the Road Traffic (NHS Charges) Act 1999 was discharged; (b) if the certificate has been reviewed, the date the certificate was confirmed or a fresh certificate was issued; or (c) the date of any agreement to treat an earlier compensation payment as having been made in final discharge of a claim made by or in respect of a traffic casualty and arising out of the injury or death
appeal against a certificate of recoverable benefits under section 11 of the Social Security (Recovery of Benefits) Act 1997	one month after the latest of – (a) the date on which any payment to the Secretary of State required under section 6 of the Social Security (Recovery of Benefits) Act 1997 was made; (b) if the certificate has been reviewed, the date the certificate was confirmed or a fresh certificate was issued; or (c) the date of any agreement to treat an earlier compensation payment as having been made in final discharge of a claim made by or in respect of an injured person and arising out of the accident, injury or disease
appeal under the Vaccine Damage Payments Act 1979	no time limit
appeal under the Tax Credits Act 2002	as set out in the Tax Credits Act 2002
appeal under the Child Trust Funds Act 2004	as set out in the Child Trust Funds Act 2004
appeal against a decision in respect of a claim for child benefit or guardian's allowance under section 12 of the Social Security Act 1998	as set out in regulation 28 of the Child Benefit and Guardian's Allowance (Decisions and Appeals) Regulations 2003

SCHEDULE 2 ISSUES IN RELATION TO WHICH THE TRIBUNAL MAY REFER A PERSON FOR MEDICAL EXAMINATION UNDER SECTION 20(2) OF THE SOCIAL SECURITY ACT 1998

Rule 25(3)

An issue falls within this Schedule if the issue –

(a) is whether the claimant satisfies the conditions for entitlement to –

(i) an attendance allowance specified in section 64 and 65(1) of the Social Security Contributions and Benefits Act 1992;

(ii) severe disablement allowance under section 68 of that Act;

(iii) the care component of a disability living allowance specified in section 72(1) and (2) of that Act;

(iv) the mobility component of a disability living allowance specified in section 73(1), (8) and (9) of that Act; or

(v) a disabled person's tax credit specified in section 129(1)(b) of that Act.

(b) relates to the period throughout which the claimant is likely to satisfy the conditions for entitlement to an attendance allowance or a disability living allowance;

(c) is the rate at which an attendance allowance is payable;

(d) is the rate at which the care component or the mobility component of a disability living allowance is payable;

(e) is whether a person is incapable of work for the purposes of the Social Security Contributions and Benefits Act 1992;

(f) relates to the extent of a person's disablement and its assessment in accordance with Schedule 6 to the Social Security Contributions and Benefits Act 1992;

(g) is whether the claimant suffers a loss of physical or mental faculty as a result of the relevant accident for the purposes of section 103 of the Social Security Contributions and Benefits Act 1992;

(h) relates to any payment arising under, or by virtue of a scheme having effect under, section 111 of, and Schedule 8 to, the Social Security Contributions and Benefits Act 1992 (workmen's compensation);

(i) is whether a person has limited capability for work or work-related activity for the purposes of the Welfare Reform Act 2007.

Appendix 4
CRIMINAL INJURIES COMPENSATION – PRACTICE STATEMENTS AND PROTOCOLS

FIRST TIER TRIBUNAL
CRIMINAL INJURIES COMPENSATION

PRACTICE GUIDANCE CI-1

Claims for financial loss – loss of earnings, loss of earning capacity, special expenses, state benefits, pension payments

1. All Appellants and their representatives are reminded that they have to prove their claim.
2. Appellants must promptly:
   - inform the Criminal Injuries Compensation Authority (the Authority) of the basis of their financial loss claim and
   - provide the Authority with all documents in support of the claim for financial loss,
   - keep the Authority informed of any changes.
3. Appellants are responsible for providing to the Authority the full name, address and other contact details of former and current employer, details of all relevant social security, pension and other benefits that have to be taken into account under paragraphs 45-48 of the Scheme and that have been and are currently in payment, and the address of all Benefits Agency etc. offices administering such payments.
4. **An employed earner** should produce the following documents:
   - legible copy of all pay slips on a weekly/monthly basis (depending on whether the applicant is paid weekly or monthly) commencing 12 months before the date of the incident, and continuing to the date when the claim ceases and (if not shown on the pay slips), proof from the employer of the date and amounts of any relevant pay rate changes, OR (if these pay slips are no longer available)
   - a letter or schedule signed by a responsible officer of the employer giving details on a weekly or monthly basis of (i) applicant's gross earnings, (ii) deductions (separately shown) in respect of the applicant's income tax, national insurance and superannuation payments for the period commencing 1 year before the date of the incident, together with all relevant pay rate changes.
5. **A self employed earner** should produce the following documents:
   - a certified copy of accounts for the 3 full tax years preceding the date of incident, continuing to the end of the year in which the claim ceases AND
   - copies of all tax returns and confirmation from Inland Revenue to show applicant's gross income, income tax and national insurance payments for these periods
6. If the Appellant and/or the Authority consider that a specialist report is required in connection with a claim for financial loss, they are referred to Practice Statement CI-3 'Commissioning specialist evidence'.
7. (Unless the hearing is solely to determine an issue on eligibility), no later than 2 weeks before the hearing date of the appeal, the Appellant and the Authority will have sought

to agree the financial loss claim on an arithmetical basis (subject always to the Tribunal's determinations on eligibility, causation and scrutiny) and will inform the Tribunal of areas of disagreement between them.

8. *An Appellant who fails to comply with this direction risks having the claim for financial loss struck out either in full or in part, and/or having an award withheld or reduced under paragraph 13(c) of the Scheme for failing to give reasonable assistance in connection with the application.*

ROGER GOODIER
Principal Judge
3 November 2008

PRACTICE STATEMENT CI-2

Listing of appeal hearings – eligibility issues

1. Where, following the response to the Notice of Appeal from the Criminal Injuries Compensation Authority (the Respondent in the appeal), the Tribunal is satisfied that an oral hearing is required to determine whether or not the Applicant is eligible under the relevant Scheme to an award of compensation, the appeal will be listed for hearing for determination on eligibility on the first available date after one month from the date of the Authority's response.
2. At the hearing, the tribunal may refuse to admit an eligibility issue not previously raised by the Authority unless good cause is shown for the delay in raising it or there is new evidence or a change in circumstances.
3. At the hearing on eligibility, if the Tribunal decides that the Appellant is eligible to an award of compensation, it will proceed to assess compensation at that hearing only if there is sufficient evidence fairly so to do – if not, it will adjourn and give directions.

Roger Goodier
Principal Judge
3 November 2008

PRACTICE STATEMENT CI-3

Specialist evidence

Commissioning specialist evidence

1. Where both the Appellant* and the Criminal Injuries Compensation Authority (the Authority) agree that a specialist report is necessary, the specialist will be jointly instructed and the specialist's reasonable fee will be paid by the Authority.
2. Save in exceptional circumstances, the Tribunal will not normally direct the Authority to reimburse to an Appellant any fee or part of a fee paid by or on behalf of the Appellant to a specialist where the Appellant has not given notice to the Authority of the intention to commission a report from a specialist and has not sought to agree with the Authority the need for the relevant report and the identity of the specialist to be instructed.
3. Where the Authority and Appellant do not agree on the need for a report from a specialist or the identity of the specialist from whom such report should be commissioned, they will make written application to the Tribunal for directions.

*The term 'Appellant' in this direction shall be deemed to include Appellant's representative where there is one.

Disclosure of specialist evidence

4. Failure by or on behalf of the Appellant promptly or at all to disclose to the Authority and the Tribunal any specialist report in the possession of the Appellant relating directly or indirectly to the relevant injury may result in the Tribunal not admitting such evidence and/or striking out a part of or the whole of a claim or deciding to withhold or reduce an award under paragraph 13(c) of the Scheme (failure to give reasonable assistance in connection with the application).

Roger Goodier
Principal Judge
3 November 2008

PRACTICE GUIDANCE CI-4

Cap on loss of earnings

Criminal Injuries Compensation Schemes – paragraph 14(a) of the 1990 Scheme; paragraph 34 of the 1996, 2001 and 2008 Schemes

The maximum amount that can be awarded for loss of earnings under the Schemes is currently £718.50 per week (£37,362 per annum).

This follows publication on 14 November 2008 by the Office for National Statistics (ONS) of the 2008 Annual Survey of Hours and Earnings (ASHE) which shows that the median weekly pay for full time employees is £479 per week. ASHE does not give details of gross average industrial earnings.

The limit of 'one and a half times the gross average industrial earnings' is prescribed at paragraph 14(a) of the 1990 Scheme and paragraph 34 of the 1996, 2001 and 2008 Schemes.

As a rule of thumb, an applicant's gross income will have to be more than £52,250 per annum before the cap will be relevant.

Roger Goodier
Principal Judge
21 November 2008

PRACTICE STATEMENT CI-5

Listing of appeal hearings; postponement of hearings

Background

1. When a date for an oral appeal hearing has been fixed, parties notified, witnesses invited and a Hearing Panel appointed, a postponement causes wasted resources and delays to hearings of other appeals. Compliance with this Practice Statement is essential to avoid delays and wasted resources and is generally in the interests of justice.
2. Definition of 'postponement' and 'adjournment':
   - postponement – where, before the hearing has commenced, a case is taken out of the list – this can be on or before the date fixed for the hearing;
   - adjournment – where, after the hearing has commenced, the Panel decides that, for whatever reason, the appeal cannot be finalised and has to put off making a final decision to another date.

Obligation to keep the Tribunal informed of any 'dates to avoid'

3. Following confirmation by the Tribunal that an oral hearing for the appeal has been granted, all parties must inform the Tribunal in writing and with reasons of any hearing dates they wish to avoid. Save in exceptional circumstances, the unavailability of a particular representative or Appellant's work commitments will not be accepted as a valid reason to postpone a hearing.

The Tribunal's listing policy

4. A case will be listed for oral hearing as soon as possible after:
   - both the Criminal Injuries Compensation Authority (the Authority) and Appellant have provided within the time permitted under the First-tier (Social Entitlement) Rules 2008 or other case management directions issued in a particular case all documents ready for the appeal hearing or;
   - (of its own motion or following a request made by the Authority or Appellant), the Tribunal gives notice that the appeal will be listed for an oral hearing or oral directions hearing.
5. The Tribunal will consider on its merits a written request to avoid a particular date or dates that has been made in compliance with paragraph 3 above.
6. The length of time before a case is listed for hearing will depend on issues such as:
   - the frequency of sittings at the particular hearings venue;
   - the number of other appeals awaiting a hearing at that venue;
   - the availability of relevant witnesses whose oral evidence has been identified as likely to assist the panel who will hear and decide the appeal;
   - any other factors considered by the Tribunal to be relevant.
7. The tribunal will give at least 14 days notice of the hearing, unless a party has agreed to accept shorter notice.
8. Once notice of the hearing has been given, the presumption will be that the Tribunal will refuse a postponement request. Only where there are compellingly good reasons for the late postponement request will the hearing be postponed in advance of the hearing date.

Applications to postpone hearings – before the date of the hearing

9. An application before the hearing date to postpone an oral hearing (including an oral directions hearing) must be made in writing addressed to The Tribunals Service – Criminal Injures Compensation at Wellington House, 134-136 Wellington Street, Glasgow G2 2XL It must be made at the earliest possible time, include all reasons for the postponement request and be supported by appropriate documentary evidence, e.g. a medical certificate.
10. A hearing date will remain effective until such time as the Tribunal notifies the parties that a postponement request has been granted. Unless the Tribunal has informed the parties that a postponement request has been granted, all concerned should proceed on the basis that the hearing will go ahead on the stated date. It must not be assumed that a postponement application will be granted, even if the Authority and Appellant both support a postponement request.

Applications to postpone hearings – on the day of the hearing

11. An application to postpone made on the day of the hearing will be considered by the panel appointed to hear the appeal. The Panel will decide whether to postpone the hearing taking the above-mentioned considerations into account.

Power to proceed in absence of a party

12. If a party fails to attend a hearing, the Tribunal may proceed with the hearing and make a final decision.

Directions

13. A Tribunal Judge or Member, or a panel at a hearing, may at any time give directions for the future progress of the appeal.

Roger Goodier
Principal Judge
3 November 2008

PRACTICE AND GUIDANCE STATEMENT CI-6

Appeals on error of law against final decision of the Tribunal

None of the tariff based Schemes and the Rules applicable to decisions made by the First-tier Tribunal in this jurisdiction provide for a final decision of the Tribunal to be reviewed, appealed, amended or otherwise interfered with, apart from

(i) the right to apply for re-instatement (a) where proceedings, or part of them, have been struck out (Rule 8(5)-(7)) or (b) where proceedings or part of them have been withdrawn (Rule 17(4));
(ii) the right to apply for a decision to be reconsidered at a hearing where the Tribunal makes a decision which disposes of proceedings without a hearing, other than decisions to which Rule 27(5) apply (Rule 27(4));
(iii) the right to apply for a rehearing where the tribunal proceeded with a hearing in a party's absence (Rule 31);
(iv) the correction of a clerical or other accidental slip or omission in a decision (Rule 36);
(v) the right to apply for a decision, or part of a decision, to be set aside subject to certain conditions (Rule 37).

Other than these above-mentioned specific exceptions, the only legal remedy open to an appellant who wishes to challenge the final decision of the Tribunal in this jurisdiction is to apply to bring judicial review proceedings of the decision:

- (in respect of incidents occurring and decisions made in England & Wales) to the Upper Tribunal*, or
- (in respect of incidents and decisions made in Scotland) to the Outer House of the Court of Session on the grounds that the decision was '**erroneous in law**'.

Parties who are contemplating making application to bring judicial review proceedings should follow the guidance below.

1. (Unless the Tribunal has already provided a full written statement of reasons for the decision), as soon as possible and in any event no later than 1 month after notification of the final decision, a party must make a written request for a full statement of reasons for the decision complained about, addressed to The Tribunals Service – Criminal Injuries, Wellington House, 134–136 Wellington Street, Glasgow G2 2XL. The request must quote the name of the appellant and the Tribunal's full case reference.
2. A party contemplating making an application to bring judicial review proceedings is requested without delay to provide to the First-tier Tribunal at the address above, written details of the alleged error of law, and all facts and matters relied on in support of the alleged error. The First-tier Tribunal's Principal Judge or nominated Tribunal Judge will scrutinise the allegation and, where satisfied that it is appropriate to do so in accordance with the paragraphs 36 or 37 of the Tribunal Procedure (First-tier Tribunal) (Social Entitlement Chamber) Rules 2008, will consider correcting or setting aside the decision or part of it.
3. Without prejudice to the above two paragraphs, the burden is on the dissatisfied party to make application to bring judicial review proceedings in accordance with applicable Upper Tribunal or Court of Session Rules.

Where incident occurred in Scotland and any hearing took place in Scotland

4. Application for judicial review must be made to the Outer House of the Court of Session, Court of Session, Parliament House, Parliament Square, Edinburgh EH1 1RQ in accordance with Chapter 58 of the Rules of the Court of Session. Note that whilst there is no prescribed time limit for lodging an application for judicial review in Scotland, objections may be taken if there is undue delay in lodging a petition.

Where the claimant lives in England or Wales, the incident occurred in England or Wales and any hearing took place in England or Wales

5. Any application for judicial review must be made in accordance with Rule 27 of the Tribunal Procedure (Upper Tribunal) Rules 2008 S.I. 2008/2698) on a prescribed claim form JR1. The time limit is 3 months after the date of the decision complained of, or 1 month after the date written reasons were given or the applicant was notified that an application for the setting aside of the decision had been unsuccessful, whichever period ends latest. The applicant may apply for an extension of time to the Upper Tribunal but must give reasons. The address of the Upper Tribunal is: The Upper Tribunal (Administrative Appeals Chamber), 5th floor Chichester Rents, 81 Chancery Lane, London WC2A 1DD. If the claimant lives in Wales or any hearing was in Wales, the application may be sent or delivered to: The Upper Tribunal (Wales), Columbus House, Langstone Business Park, Chepstow Road, Newport NP18 2LX. The application form JR1 may be obtained from the London Office or on its website **www.administrativeappeals.tribunals.gov.uk**.

Where the case has connections with both Scotland and England & Wales

6. An application to bring judicial review proceedings may be made to whichever of the Court of Session or the Upper Tribunal is more appropriate in the circumstances of the case, having particular regard to the convenience of the parties and the issues arising on the application for judicial review. The other party or parties may object to the choice made by the applicant but it should be borne in mind that the Upper Tribunal may sit in Scotland as well as in England and Wales and that the Court of Session may refer a case to the Upper Tribunal who would then be able to hear it in either Scotland or England & Wales.

Correct Defendant and address for service

7. The Defendant in all judicial review proceedings in tariff based Scheme cases is First-tier Tribunal; the address for service is The Tribunals Service, Criminal Injuries, Wellington House, 134–136 Wellington Street, Glasgow G2 2XL. Applications for judicial review in tariff based Scheme cases served at any other address will not be accepted. An appellant should consider joining the Criminal Injuries Compensation Authority as a Defendant or Interested Party. Where there is a challenge to a tariff based Scheme itself, the appellant will need to consider whether to add as Defendant the Secretary of State for the Ministry of Justice.

14 May 2009

Roger Goodier
Principal Judge
Social Entitlement Chamber – criminal injuries compensation.

[*Pursuant to Order of Lord Chief Justice of England and Wales – classes of cases specified under section 18(6) of the Tribunals and Courts and Enforcement Act 2007 (the 2007 Act) – direction in relation to an application made to the High Court of Upper Tribunal on or after 3 November 2008 that seeks relief of a kind mentioned in section 15(1) of the 2007 Act; direction that the following classes of case are specified for the purposes of section 18(6) of the 2007 Act:

(a) any decision of the First-Tier Tribunal on an appeal made in exercise of a right conferred by the Criminal Injuries Compensation Scheme in compliance with section 5 of the Criminal Injuries Compensation Act 1995 (appeals against decisions on review);
(b) any decision of the First-Tier Tribunal made under Tribunal Procedure Rules or section 9 of the 2007 Act where there is no right of appeal to the Upper Tribunal and that decision is not an excluded decision within paragraph (b), (c), or (f) of section 11(5) of the 2007 Act.]

PRACTICE DIRECTION
FIRST TIER AND UPPER TRIBUNAL

Child, vulnerable adult and sensitive witnesses

1. In this Practice Direction:
   (a) 'child' means a person who has not attained the age of 18;
   (b) 'vulnerable adult' has the same meaning as in the Safeguarding Vulnerable Groups Act 2006;
   (c) 'sensitive witness' means an adult witness where the quality of evidence given by the witness is likely to be diminished by reason of fear or distress on the part of the witness in connection with giving evidence in the case.

Circumstances under which a child, vulnerable adult or sensitive witness may give evidence

2. A child, vulnerable adult or sensitive witness will only be required to attend as a witness and give evidence at a hearing where the Tribunal determines that the evidence is necessary to enable the fair hearing of the case and their welfare would not be prejudiced by doing so.
3. In determining whether it is necessary for a child, vulnerable adult or sensitive witness to give evidence to enable the fair hearing of a case the Tribunal should have regard to all the available evidence and any representations made by the parties.
4. In determining whether the welfare of the child, vulnerable adult or sensitive witness would be prejudiced it may be appropriate for the Tribunal to invite submissions from interested persons, such as a child's parents.
5. The Tribunal may decline to issue a witness summons under the Tribunal Procedure Rules or to permit a child, vulnerable adult or sensitive witness to give evidence where it is satisfied that the evidence is not necessary to enable the fair hearing of the case and must decline to do so where the witness's welfare would be prejudiced by them giving evidence.

Manner in which evidence is given

6. The Tribunal must consider how to facilitate the giving of any evidence by a child, vulnerable adult or sensitive witness.
7. It may be appropriate for the Tribunal to direct that the evidence should be given by telephone, video link or other means directed by the Tribunal, or to direct that a person be appointed for the purpose of the hearing who has the appropriate skills or experience in facilitating the giving of evidence by a child, vulnerable adult or sensitive witness.
8. This Practice Direction is made by the Senior President of Tribunals with the agreement of the Lord Chancellor. It is made in the exercise of powers conferred by the Tribunals, Courts and Enforcement Act 2007.

INDEX